Do the Best You ~~Can~~ CAN'T!

Bud Stumbaugh

ARCHWAY
PUBLISHING

Archway Publishing books may be ordered through booksellers or by contacting:

Archway Publishing
1663 Liberty Drive
Bloomington, IN 47403
www.archwaypublishing.com
844-669-3957

Artist Credit: The Dahlonega Nugget

Unless otherwise noted, scripture taken from the King James Version of the Bible.

Scripture quotations marked (RSV) are from Revised Standard Version of the Bible, copyright © 1946, 1952, and 1971 National Council of the Churches of Christ in the United States of America. Used by permission. All rights reserved worldwide.

ISBN: 978-1-6657-2127-1 (sc)
ISBN: 978-1-6657-2125-7 (hc)
ISBN: 978-1-6657-2126-4 (e)

Library of Congress Control Number: 2022906563

Print information available on the last page.

Archway Publishing rev. date: 04/20/2022

DEDICATION

For my daughters and their spouses: Stacey and Jerry and Susan and Jack

For my grandkids: Stacey's gift; Mr. Noah and Ms. Ava and Susan's gift; Mr. Ellis and Mr. Robert

In the hope that you will go to sleep, wake up, dream—in that order. After all, the time to dream is when you are awake and in full control of your mental and physical faculties. Really meaningful action items take place when you are bright-eyed, clear-minded and mentally sharp, not zonked out.

So, loves of my life, don't waste dreams during hours made for snoring. Have vivid visions when wide awake. Then, to make your dreams come true, remember to practice the principles you've heard me speak about almost all your lives and that I have now put in writing and dedicated to each of you.

Dad/Granddaddy/Bud

CONTENTS

FOREWORD

By Guy Millner, cofounder and executive chairman of AssuranceAmerica Corporation and founder and CEO of Norrell Corporation, who led its growth from zero to a $1.4 billion New York Stock Exchange company.

What a delight and honor it is to write this foreword for my friend and "serial entrepreneur," Bud Stumbaugh.

This book should be a guiding light for any person seeking success in their career or any other part of their life. It's about abundant optimism and how one can do more than they ever expected!

I connected with Lawrence (Bud) Stumbaugh in the early '70s when he was the Atlanta manager for a well-respected New York recruiting firm. I called Bud and asked him in our first meeting if he would join my company and help build a national recruiting organization. Bud accepted, and after just six years with us, his organization had twenty-five branches in the Southeast and Southwest.

We officed in a small two-story building and would meet and have great discussions (always positive!) before the day started for others. In Bud's book, he references Dr. Norman Vincent Peale's book on positive thinking. Hey, Bud could have written it! He certainly lives it.

Bud puts everybody else first. His voice-mail message promises he will call you back whether or not he knows you, and he follows up on that promise. I know very few people as driven to succeed as Bud, but not just for himself. If you are his friend, and he has thousands, there's nothing he won't do to help you. People teach about leadership; however, Bud exemplifies it every day. He leads by example, and there's no one more humble, yet few have his record of achievements.

Over pancakes at the Buckhead IHOP, while we were in the middle of building the recruiting organization, Bud told me he wanted to run for the Georgia Senate. He truly wanted to serve in public office. I understood that and accepted his resignation, which was a big loss for me. To achieve his goal of being elected to public office, he literally knocked on doors ten hours a day.

Bud went on to build several large businesses, sold several, and in the process achieved more than most others, yet he was never 100 percent satisfied. You see, he is always focused on future successes. And with humble beginnings as motivation, he has succeeded time and time again.

In 1997, he called me from Boston and expressed interest in returning to Atlanta to start a new company in the insurance business, asking me to be his partner. A better partner I have never had.

That partnership was the start of AssuranceAmerica, which is now the sixty-seventh largest auto insurer in the United States, with 160,000 policyholders.

ACKNOWLEDGMENTS

You've written a book, Bud. So, who cares (cared)?

The following special people cared enough about me and my goal of writing a book to share their time, insights, wisdom, opinions, expertise, common sense, judgment, and encouragement until the mission was complete. And they did this without complaining or calling me a nuisance, even though I nonstop took advantage of their willing spirits and ever-present patience. I'm not capable of articulating an ample amount of appreciation. But, believe me, my gratitude is gargantuan.

Tania Stumbaugh—My wife's first language is Portuguese, but she nonetheless devoured every word I wrote in English and gave me feedback that improved the message I was trying to compose. Then, because I am from the old school that uses red ink to mark-up and edit paper copies of my typed documents, she printed and reprinted each edited version time and time again at all hours of the day and night without ever fussing or frowning.

Stacey Andrick—My daughter read every chapter after hard days at her demanding job and told me what kept her awake or put her to sleep. The sleep assessments motivated me to make meaningful changes so you, dear reader, can keep your eyes wide open.

Susan Irwin—My daughter performed the technical tasks of automating the numbering of pages, positioning paragraphs properly, setting margins to book-size widths and lengths, and then formatting the finished document so it met the publisher's submission requirements. Credit for coming up with the front-cover design is also due this dear daughter.

Carole Hollingsworth—I look up to the mother of my two daughters because she is one of the most decent and caring people in the world. She read each chapter and told me how I might phrase words more sensitively and less offensively, and she was especially helpful in making the verbiage more inclusive of folks who might be different from me.

Guy Millner—My friend and business partner is one of the people briefly featured in this book. More than anyone, he encouraged me to put pen to paper to describe what he had seen me practice in my life in general and in businesses in which he was majority shareholder. Before a word was written, he committed to purchasing quantities of the finished product to give to his family, friends, and multitude of business partners, affiliates and associates.

Matt Aiken—As editor and publisher of my hometown newspaper, *The Dahlonega Nugget*, Matt's down-to-earth, colorful, folksy writing style is comparable to that of *New York Times* best-selling author and humorist Lewis Grizzard, a good ole Georgia boy who died in 1994. If I was wiser, I'd have hired Matt to ghostwrite this book. But I was doggedly determined to do it myself. As a result, Matt only made editorial suggestions that eliminated some redundancies and helped me find a shorter, not so boring route to the point I wanted to make. If there are still some boring parts to my book, those represent the times I didn't listen to Matt.

CHAPTER 1

NOT EVERY MOMMA CAN COOK

Just Because Someone Says It's So, Doesn't Make It So

THIS TALE'S TRUE. HOWEVER, THE name has been changed to protect against a possible bolt of lightning coming from heaven straight to my computer as I type this. You see, my friend Steve Busbee's dear, departed momma might be miffed at my message.

Steve and I were driving down a busy street looking for a place to have lunch. One restaurant had a neon sign signaling, "Just like momma's home cooking." Upon my suggesting we stop at this local establishment, Steve told me he missed his wonderful momma, but not her cooking. "Momma couldn't boil water without burning it. If the food at that place tastes like Momma's, let's get at least a mile away from it."

The point of the above story is that Mom, as wonderful and wise as she is, should not always be seen as the ultimate, end-all example of excellence. The same goes with Dad. Or your preacher. Or your third-grade homeroom teacher, Mrs. Brooks. (Sorry, Mrs. Brooks.) After all, even the best of the best are not perfect. They are not always the greatest in a given area. They have faults. They sometimes make mistakes. They occasionally set less-than-positive examples. They sometimes give bad advice. They are not always the epitome of wisdom. They sometimes have flawed philosophies. What they say "ain't" necessarily so.

A well-known quotation from either Ben Franklin or Edgar Allen Poe (historians disagree about who said it first) makes the point better than the preceding paragraph: "Believe none of what you hear and only half of what you see." Famous baseball player and street-smart dispenser of delightful ditties, Yogi Berra, said it more colorfully. "It's not what we don't know that gets us in trouble; it's what we know for sure that just ain't so."

Realizing that some of the things we've been taught all our lives and know for sure "just ain't so," I've challenged convention and consensus in this book. Hopefully, my questioning of so many sayings—especially the last one—won't see me sentenced like Socrates. His views often contradicted everyday citizens and certainly conflicted with those in control. His failure to agree with the authorities in Athens finally led to heaping helpings of hemlock. The charge was "corrupting youth by questioning tradition." No matter what befalls me as a result of my treatment of tradition, just like Socrates, I intend to remain doggedly determined until I die!

How many of the following fables or falsehoods were fostered on us by Momma or others we thought were infallibly good guidance givers? Is it too harsh to use the word "falsehoods" in the same sentence in which I've used "fables?" After all, fables are hardly more than humorous homilies or innocuous idioms. Falsehoods, on the other hand, are often purposefully dispensed to deceive or damage. Okay, maybe less-harsh verbiage like "old wives' tales" would be a more appropriate and acceptable way to articulate the idea I'm trying to get across. However, "old wives' tales" seems to place blame only on older married females. It's just not fair to leave out younger married females. Or single females, young or old. Or young or old males who may be married or single. No matter if the fables, sayings, or philosophies I'm about to share (and slander) are called practical principles, adroit advice, or authoritative axioms by some; they are, nonetheless, falsehoods. Worse, they sometimes impart a few fears, hang-ups, and hesitations that may cause us to live life with limits that become liabilities in one's pursuit of positive outcomes.

- You've likely heard that opening an umbrella indoors brings bad luck. In mentioning this fable to my wife, who is from Brazil, she told me that some cultures outside the United States speak specifically about the kind of bad luck that occurs because of opening an umbrella inside a house. Some say that if you open an umbrella indoors, you won't be able to have children. Now, opening an umbrella around an end table full of knickknacks may increase the chance of chipping or cracking china, but there is obviously no scientific study proving that it results in faulty or failing fertility.

- We've all probably been told that it is dangerous to swim with a full stomach. When I was growing up, the rule at my house was that my sisters and I could not jump in the water until two hours after we had eaten. We had to digest our meal first. Otherwise, we would get cramps in our abdomen, the pain would restrict our movement, and we would drown. Biological and physiological research doesn't validate this view. Yet, hours of fun have been denied or delayed because of this unfounded fear followed like fact.

- Some parents and spiritual leaders who think masturbation is wrong have fostered the fiction that it causes blindness or hairy palms. Whether one thinks masturbation is a sin or normal healthy human behavior is a matter for each religion and individual to decide. However, don't you think teenagers, as well as adults, have enough stress in their lives without people with no medical or scientific expertise fabricating stories about losing one's vision or having to shave not only one's face but also hands?

- No one, unless he or she is a masochist, wants seven years of bad luck hanging over his or her head. However, one fable that has been fostered since mirrors were made has instilled just such a fear of future failure in the lives of many people. Break a mirror and you face terrible times. Seven years of sad scenarios. A number of negative years one cannot negate. Gloom and doom become a figment of imagination fixed in one's head by a fable that says accidentally dropping a piece of reflective glass brings about a future full of foibles and futility.

- Similar to the mirror myth is the warning many mommas have given about walking under a ladder. That, too, supposedly causes bad luck. A person who walks under a ladder that has a painter or carpenter on it may be in danger of an object accidentally being dropped on his or her head. However, it certainly won't cause continuing calamities after coming out from under the ladder.

- Those seeking smooth skin likely listened to this legend: toads cause warts. When I was a kid, all my friends and I knew that if we caught a frog with our bare hands, we would end up with warts. Well, that's what our mommas told us. However, warts are caused by a virus that toads don't carry or pass on. At least this fiction saved many a frog from human harassment.

- Any harm caused by the above mommas' myths is minor compared to the major medical mistakes propounded by Martin Luther's message (myth) about manure. In Luther's *Table Talk*, in his chapter titled "Of God's Works," he extols excrement's excellent healing power: "Tis wonderful how God has put such excellent physic in mere muck; we know by experience that swine's dung stints the blood; horse's serves for the pleurisy; man's heals wounds and black blotches; asses' is used for the bloody flux, and cow's with preserved roses, serves for epilepsy, or for convulsions of children." Hey, just because a famous person says it's so doesn't make it so!

The Most Limiting Language/Sorriest Saying/Cruelest Cliché of All

Not only mommas, but also dads, grandparents, godparents, brothers and sisters, aunts and uncles, schoolteachers, preachers, coaches, counselors, motivational speakers, doctors, advisors, friends, neighbors, and every living person above the age of three have given this guidance. You have repeated it to others and even to yourself many, many times. I have often said it too (though it was in the distant past and I'll never say it again in the future). The saying is so sacrosanct that you may think I'm crazy to call this cliché in question. However, it is so confining that it cannot be correct counsel to contribute to anyone for whom you have care and concern.

The cliché that Momma and the rest of us so freely and frequently use, and that I call the cruelest cliché and sorriest saying is: "Do the best you can."

Oh, such limiting language. You see, if you and I only do the best we can, it leaves no room for stretching beyond what is the norm for us. It inhibits improvements. It says staying stuck in the status quo is satisfactory. It deters us from daring to do the daunting. It allows the accepted to be acceptable. Fearless feats are forever out of favor. Challenges to correctness cease. What has always been will always be. Breaking outside the box that we or others have built will never begin.

Doing the best you can may help you fit in, but it won't help you stand out. Doing no more than the best you can dooms you to being one *of* a million, instead of one *in* a million.

If we only do the best we *can*, then how do we conquer the following *can'ts*?

I can't quit smoking. I can't swim. I can't remember names. I can't get a promotion. I can't keep a secret. I can't speak in front of an audience. I can't ride my bicycle 100 miles each weekend. I can't cook. I can't jog a mile. I can't afford college. I can't find time to take my kids bowling. I can't start a business. I can't save 10 percent of my income. I can't build rapport with my neighbor. I can't balance my checkbook. I can't forgive him/her for_____. I can't learn a foreign language. I can't control my temper. I can't quit abusing alcohol. I can't get along with my in-laws. I can't grow flowers. I can't save my marriage. I can't apologize. I can't drive a stick shift. I can't tie a tie. I can't climb a mountain. I can't earn a living. I can't read one book a month. I can't control my children. I can't buy a house. I can't relax. I can't sew. I can't quit my job. I can't get over_____. I can't stop using foul language. I can't make all As and Bs. I can't lose weight. I can't take a chance on_____.

Let's modify the message to: "Do the best you can't!" It's the attitude and frame of mind that will help you devise a plan and determine a path to overcome the long list of can'ts above as well as any other can'ts in your life that may not be on the above list.

In this book, you will find examples of those who did the best they can't. You'll read about people that achieved the unachievable and did what they or others thought can't be done. Some became rich and famous by doing what they or others thought was impossible. However, like most of us reading this book, most of my examples are not about famous people. They are relatively unknown. But, by doing what they could not do, they enhanced their effectiveness, increased their influence, and heightened their happiness. And they serve to show that you, too, can do the best you can't.

Even if you have only average talent, physical or emotional handicaps, a low IQ, an inferior education, were abused in some way, came from a broken home, have financial stress, or receive no encouragement and positive reinforcement for what you want to do, you can still do the best you can't. The examples in this book are proof positive!

You will find principles, programs, and plans in this book that have been tested over time and proven to be true and trustworthy in achieving what was, at least at first appearance, apparently not attainable. They have certainly helped this old boy who grew up on the wrong side of the tracks, socially and economically, to do the best he can't. If you, too, will put these principles, programs, and plans into practice, you will exceed any expectations Momma ever expressed.

CHAPTER 2

EVERYBODY KNOWS CHRIS

He (and Others) Did the Best They
Couldn't, So Why Not You Too?

Perhaps a disclaimer is in order, lest you think I look up to, think highly of, and respect all facets of Chris' life. I do not. And while daring to do what couldn't be done is an excellent example to emulate, that's not true of many of his actions, which include pillaging, plundering, trade trickery, and worse. I trust your moral compass can discern which of Chris' examples to revere and which to reject. That's the case with each person about whom I write.

So, who is Chris? Well, smart, straight "A" standouts know Chris. Feeble "F" failures also know Chris. He is so famous today that even the most awful at academics remember this part of our schooling. Chris is currently acclaimed as an accomplished commander. But centuries ago, his colleagues considered Chris crazy and cautioned him, "You can't."

You will recall the year he countered his critics. It was 1492, and at least one man believed the world was round, not flat. He had faith that he could sail west to get east. Of course, most imagined it impossible. So many skillful seamen were such scared skeptics that it was difficult to secure seasoned sailors to set sail. Yet, Columbus raised the funds and found the fearless few to help him navigate the unknown. Now "crazy Chris" is forever famous. All because he didn't do the best he could. Instead, he did the best he couldn't—or, at least, the best others thought he couldn't.

Christopher Columbus' long-ago daunting derring-do reminds me of another impossible trip, this one made in the twentieth century. Momma declared that no man would ever set foot on the moon. After all, she said, "If God had meant for man to be on the moon, he would have put him there." Despite her dismissive declaration, the faraway feat became a finished fiat on July 21, 1969.

Years before that, two brothers, Orville and Wilbur, did what they couldn't do—fly an object heavier than air. Figuratively or literally, what impossible trip might you take that others tell you can't be traveled? Later chapters will outline the steps to follow if you want to take such a journey of doing what seems impossible—doing the "best you can't."

Despite my momma's misgivings, many, maybe even a majority in the engineering, aviation, and scientific world believed President Kennedy's stated goal of landing an American on the moon was doable. However, just six short years prior to Kennedy's 1960 announcement about America's aeronautical ambitions, a much more widespread society of scientists was almost unanimous in their belief that, while man could fly to the moon, there was one thing a human could never do.

Medical doctors and experts in kinesiology, anatomy, physics, zoology, and biodynamics pretty much all agreed that the human body could not run a sub-4-minute mile. Gunder Hagg of Sweden had come the closest with his world record time of 4 minutes and 1.3 seconds in

1945. Time and time again, he tried to break his on record. He could never even match it. Others tried and miserably missed the mark. Consensus in the coaching community was that it couldn't be accomplished. However, all their naysaying couldn't convince a 25-year-old British medical student at Oxford University that he couldn't beat Hagg's time. The future doctor had run a mile in a gold-medal time of 4 minutes and 4.1 seconds. Notwithstanding this fantastically fast feat, he was told, "you certainly can't" improve your own time by the 4.2 seconds needed to get below 4 minutes.

It was May 6, 1954. About three thousand spectators had assembled at Iffley Road Track in Oxford, England, to watch a match between the Amateur Athletic Association and Oxford University Athletic Club. Roger Bannister, the above-mentioned medical student, had carefully planned the race. He had asked Chris Brasher and Chris Chataway to aid him as pacemakers. Brasher's role was to be the first pacemaker and set a torrid pace that Brasher was not capable of continuing for an entire mile. When Brasher tired, Bannister signaled for Chataway, who was in third place, to move up. He did so with a burst of speed that he could maintain only until about two hundred yards from the finish line. Then, Bannister, with a shot of adrenaline his mind and muscle mustered, sprinted across the finish line as if it was a hundred-yard dash. The time: 3 minutes and 59.4 seconds! In subsequent chapters, I'll feature some keys to success that led to Bannister's achieving the "can't be done" sub-4-minute mile. No matter the impossibilities you'd like to achieve, these same keys are critical if you are going to do the best you can't.

For now, though, here are some after-occurrences to Bannister's feat that you should find interesting and inspiring. Just six weeks after Roger Bannister did what couldn't be done, an Australian, John Landy, ran the mile in a new world record time of 3 minutes and 57.9 seconds. Later, a kid from Wichita, Kansas, became the first high school athlete to run a sub-4-minute mile. It was 1965 and Jim Ryun, a high school junior, set a track-meet record of 3 minutes and

55.3 seconds. In 1966, he set a new world record of 3 minutes and 51.3 seconds. In 1967, he broke his own world record with a time of 3 minutes and 51.1 seconds. Today's record time for the mile is held by Moroccan Hicham El Guerrouj. He achieved his time of 3 minutes and 43.13 seconds in July 1999, and it will likely never be surpassed. Not because it "can't" be done, but because the mile run is no longer a part of the Olympics or other major track contests. It has been replaced by the 1,500-meter run.

A name better known than Bannister's, and probably right up there (pun intended) with Neil Armstrong's, the man who first stepped on soil outside our own solar sands, is that of Rosa Parks from Montgomery, Alabama. As a student at Albert G. Parrish High School in Selma, Alabama, in the mid-1950s, I knew Montgomery pretty well. I traveled the fifty miles from Selma to Montgomery to play football and baseball against Sidney Lanier and Robert E. Lee High Schools domiciled there. I knew, and Rosa Parks also knew, if you were Black, "you couldn't" ride in the front of the bus in Montgomery. Selma had the same segregated seating system. At that time in America, segregation was legal. Not moral, but legal.

Knowing the end result would be arrest, jail time, and losing her way of earning a living, and maybe even losing her life, Rosa Parks faced what almost all others would have felt was futile. By doing what a Black person couldn't do, sitting in front of the bus, Rosa Parks set in motion a movement that motivated a then unknown Black man to lead it. Dr. Martin Luther King, Jr., may never have led our nation and other parts of the world to better practice the "Golden Rule" of treating others the way one wants to be treated if he had not felt empowered by her example.

Shame on me that I never once thought back then that if Black people had the same amount of money to pay for bus fare that I had, they ought to have as much right to choose a seat in the front of the bus as I had. Logic, common sense, and the Golden Rule should have made this obvious to me. But, instead of personally pushing to overcome obvious oppression, it was an unlikely little lady who did what she was told "she couldn't" do. Thankfully, she did more than the best she could!

If Christopher Columbus, Roger Bannister, and Rosa Parks did what could not be done, why can't you do the best you can't? Oh, you protest, these were famous people and I'm just little ole me who's not even known by my neighbor three doors down the street. That may be true. But remember, these now-famous people did not become so until after they did what couldn't be done. And if you will be motivated to do the best you can't only by less known, or totally unknown "common, regular, normal, everyday Janes and Johns like you," there are plenty of those who have done and are continuing to do the best they can't. So read on and be motivated.

Steve Welker

My friend Steve Welker is an encouraging example of someone who has done (is doing) the best he can't. A few years ago, he and his wife, Kristi, were driving north from their home in Scottsdale to the Phoenix airport when they saw a southbound car driving toward them while being followed by a police vehicle with its siren sounding and lights flashing. As was the sensible and legal thing to do, Steve drove his car off the roadway—so much so that he stopped with his tires resting somewhat on the sidewalk. Surely, he would be safely out of the path of the police pursuit. Or so Steve surmised.

Unfortunately, the oncoming vehicle veered to the left, jumped the median at sixty miles an hour, flew through the air, and crashed headlong into Steve's Jeep Cherokee, which was catapulted into the air and rolled over three terrible times. Steve's head was impacted by his jeep's steering column, which had been shoved upward, the roof, which had been shoved downward, and the dashboard, which had shattered inward. Virtually every bone in his face was broken, his brain badly battered, and his eyes enormously injured.

Doctors at the surgical intensive care unit of the emergency hospital where Steve was taken told his family he probably would not live through the next twenty-four hours, but if he did, he might have to start life like he was a baby again. That meant he would have to once more learn to talk, walk, feed himself, and perform other routine activities. According to his doctors, Steve's future likely included lifelong physical and mental impairments.

Here's where Steve's story takes a turn for the better. Because of the mighty medical measures administered to Steve, along with his grit, guts, hard work, faith, encouragement from his family, and, most of all, Kristi's constant concern and care, Steve turned out physically and mentally "normal." Well, with one exception. He was blinded in both eyes as a result of his tragic trauma. Steve didn't die, but because of the impact of plastic and metal against flesh and bone and the resulting intracranial swelling, his optic nerve did die. Steve was left totally and permanently blind. In a matter of a few chaotic seconds, Steve's world was plunged into complete darkness.

A few months after leaving the hospital, Steve could have settled into a sedentary style of life. Inability to see justifies becoming a couch potato. Right? Wrong!

A blind person certainly can't play golf. Right? Wrong! Steve decided to do what can't be done. He had played golf fairly often before his accident, but he says he didn't play very well. So, he might again not play well, but he decided that would not deter him from playing. He got a friend to take him to a driving range where he visualized in his mind the ball on the tee. He swung hundreds and even thousands of times until the repetition enabled him to solidly strike that small sphere. Now he was ready to do the same thing on a golf course.

Steve needs someone to verbalize direction and distance, and then he picks the proper club accordingly. By continuing to practice, he learned to drive the ball some 250 yards straight toward the green. His golf buddies tell him he has not hit a sand trap in ten years. However, he admits that some of those friends frequently fib. During one round of golf, a friend told him to stay in the cart because there was an alligator about thirty feet away. Steve says he didn't argue against the advice. And while he obviously could not see the creature's toothy snout, it did not matter, because he was carefully listening for any alligator sounds.

By the way, a blind person can't snow ski either. Right? Wrong! It was spring when Steve was blinded. That fall, Steve heard of a fellow that gave skiing lessons to the disabled. Steve had loved skiing Telluride, Colorado; Lake Tahoe, Nevada; and Park City, Utah, when he was in college. So why not use this fellow who gave skiing lessons to the disabled as a resource for returning to the slopes he loved? After Steve and a friend had practiced going down a couple of slopes with the instructor, they decided to take the chairlift to the top and try it with only the friend's assistance. A blind person needs someone in front of him or her to tell when to turn to the right or left to miss a tree, a rock, or another skier. For ten straight skiing seasons, Steve's friend has kept him from tackling a tree trunk or battering a big boulder.

In his book, *The World at My Fingertips*, Steve tells of one ski trip during which the ski patrol was bringing someone down the mountain on a sled. Usually, that means someone has had an accident and suffered a broken leg or another injury that makes it impossible to navigate back down on their own. On this occasion, however, it was a woman who got so scared of the steep slope that she could not descend it on her own. Well, Steve did not find the steep slope so scary and was able to do what a sighted skier couldn't do!

In addition to the above feats, since being blinded, Steve has been an agent in an insurance business and then became the president of his own insurance agency. He is now a motivational speaker. If you're interested in his services or if you want to buy one of his books, you may reach him at 480-730-6200 or Radicalresiliency.com. I've had Steve speak to all my company's associates, so I can vouch for his effectiveness. In fact, his presentation dealt a big blow to my ego. After Steve's speech, one of my colleagues told me it was the best she had ever heard. She had heard me give two different motivational speeches in the past. The lesson learned is that I'm no better than second best. Ouch, that hurts!

I had a chat with Steve just before I sat down to write this chapter. He was characteristically humble, despite his awe-inspiring accomplishments.

"I am an ordinary man who went through a devastating event and was able to come out on the other side," Steve said. "Prior to becoming blind, I would have thought, 'I can't do that.' I have learned never to underestimate the strength and resiliency of the human spirit."

Reader, contemplate Steve's comment next time you think you can't do something you've never done before, something beyond your current capacity, or something out of the ordinary. If Steve can, why can't you?

Rusty Redfern

Rusty Redfern gets credit (or blame, depending on how you view my time in elective politics) for helping me win my campaign for the Georgia State Senate, where I served for eight terms. He was only twelve years old at the time. His mom volunteered to stuff mailboxes with my campaign brochure. She drove from mailbox to mailbox while Rusty rode along in the passenger seat, separating brochures one by one from a stack of hundreds and then reaching out the car window to open each mailbox and place my printed piece therein.

Thanks, Rusty, for doing what would be simple for most of us but was somewhat more complex for you. You see, Rusty was what was called a Thalidomide baby.

For readers not old enough to have been around in the mid-1950s, that was when Thalidomide, an over-the-counter drug, was produced. It was marketed in more than fifty countries. An article from Northwestern University says the drug became so popular that, by 1960, just four years after it hit the market, its sales rivaled aspirin. One of its most widespread uses was for nausea and insomnia in pregnant women. While it was effective in curing those conditions, it was withdrawn from distribution in 1962. That's because, as a result of taking this drug, mothers around the world had given birth to some 10,000+ babies with phocomelia. Phocomelia is a rare condition that causes missing, shortened, and flipper-like limbs. For Rusty, this condition was real rather than rare. He was one of those born with no hands or arms.

Most of us, no matter how old or young, are familiar with the expression "the three Rs." That's reading, 'riting, 'rithmatic. The three Rs are used to denote the most basic areas of early schooling. Rusty Redfern could have easily and perhaps justifiably reduced it to "reading and 'rithmatic." After all, a person with no hands and arms can't write. Right? Wrong! A person with no hands and arms can't stuff printed pieces in mailboxes. Right? Wrong!

A person with no arms and hands can write and stuff mailboxes with his feet. Right? Right! Rusty had a choice of can or can't. He could take the path of least resistance. He could take the path of most assistance. Decide to be disabled. Or decide to be determined. Decide difficult can be done. Practically from birth, Rusty's parents encouraged him to be independent. As he got older, his inner spirit sought self-sufficiency. Rusty was determined to use his toes like you and I use fingers. Toes could learn to use a knife and fork for eating. For writing. For stuffing mailboxes.

Of course, toes can't be used to draw like a professional artist. Right? Wrong! Rusty went from "two Rs" to "three Rs," to stuffing mailboxes, to becoming a skilled artist using a technique called pointillism, developed in 1886 by the now famous Georges Seurat. Seurat had arms and hands. Rusty emulates this renown master, except, "Look, Mom, no hands." Rusty produces, illustrates, and sells a series of notecards, Christmas cards, limited-edition prints, and original drawings he creates with his toes. If you are interested in possibly acquiring some of his beautiful handiwork—um, "footiwork," that is—you can contact Rusty at redfernoriginals.com.

In the meantime, be inspired to exceed any expectations that you or others ever had of yourself by emulating Rusty's example of conquering can't. As Rusty said the last time I talked with him, "Most people figured I couldn't reach as far as those with arms and hands could reach. I was determined to reach farther than the longest arms and hands—even though I had none. 'Can't' was not going to be a part of my thinking or vocabulary."

Zack Hodskins

Zack lived in a small Georgia town with a population of 32,661. What he did generated a huge headline with two action-oriented photographs taking up almost half a page of space, plus additional space for a story in the sports section of the *New York Times*. Note, the NYT is published in a city of 8,336,817, nearly a thousand miles away from Milton, Georgia. The NYT headline traces the theme of this book. It shouted out, "Don't Tell Him He Can't."

Zack Hodskins probably had better odds of being offered the job of CEO of Georgia-headquartered Home Depot than the newsworthy offer he had just accepted. That offer guaranteed him a roster spot on the University of Florida's varsity basketball team. The reason that generated headlines was because Zack was born without the two hands normally needed to excel at basketball. He had no left hand or even a forearm.

Throughout his seventeen years of life, he had endured a lot of caustic remarks from cruel kids. Adults were frequently telling him what he couldn't do. They advised him not to push himself too hard, lest he end up disappointed and disheartened when he failed, as he surely would. But instead of letting all this beat him down, he used ridicule and doubts expressed by skeptics as steppingstones to success. Tell him he could not do something and his competitive spirit would take command. He refused to wear the slip-on shoes his mother bought him so he could avoid the difficulty of tying laces. He even competed with two-handed people to see who was fastest at tying shoes. He usually won!

A lot of people doubted Zack's athletic ability, but he did whatever it took to overcome what to others would have been a debilitating deterrence. Long after teammates had ended practice, he would stay to shoot extra hoops. Doing so without the luxury of switching hands while dribbling or shooting led to bloody fingers after many a workout that was hours longer than other kids' workouts. Allowing himself to be beat was not acceptable. Doing the best a one-handed player could was not compelling enough. He challenged himself to do the best he couldn't, not just the best he could. That got him a story in the *New York Times* and an offer to play basketball at a major university—something hundreds of thousands of two-handed Georgia kids before him never got.

Billy Payne

Another feat that couldn't be done—but was—merited another newspaper story. It was the *Atlanta Journal-Constitution* this time, and the story was some eighteen years after the feat was achieved at the 1996 Summer Olympics. The article featured an interview with Billy Payne, the fellow who came up with the idea and led the effort to bring the 1996 Summer Olympics to Atlanta.

As the world might measure success, Billy Payne had not achieved anything tremendously significant before winning and managing the Olympics for Atlanta. He was not a multi-millionaire. He was not CEO of a major company, or of a small one either. He did not hold public office. He was not a buddy of the governor or mayor. He was a nondescript and totally unheralded real estate attorney.

Before taking on the multibillion-dollar Olympics project, Billy's biggest task had been leading the fundraising campaign for a new sanctuary for his church. That undertaking gave him such a sense of satisfaction that he told his wife he just had to find another endeavor to engineer; he wanted an even bigger challenge to conquer. The very next day, he came up with the idea of bringing the 1996 Summer Olympics to Atlanta. And he would not be dissuaded by the naysayers who said it could not be done.

Atlanta started off as a real dark horse. Perhaps a laughingstock. Since this was the centennial Olympics, most everyone knew it would be awarded to Athens, Greece, the birthplace of the first games. If not Athens, then surely it would be awarded to one of the four other finalists: Toronto, Canada; Melbourne, Australia; Manchester, England; or Belgrade, Yugoslavia. This stiff competition didn't have the media critically calling them a second-tier city, a moniker they used to describe Atlanta.

Atlanta was the only city in the running that could not muster up a population of a million. It could not even break a half-million since its boundaries boasted only 478,614 citizens. Atlanta was criticized for its congestion. Its Confederate history could cripple any chances of it becoming the choice. On top of these negatives, the other competing cities spent a total of over $100 million promulgating their positives, while Atlanta spent only $7.3 million.

In the January 26, 2014 newspaper interview, Billy was asked who influenced him to think so big as to try something so bodacious. He credited his dad with instilling in him the belief that even when Billy had done his best, bigger and better possibilities may not yet have been exhausted. The *Atlanta Journal-Constitution* quoted Billy as follows: "Even though I thought I had performed well, Dad wanted me to know there was a little bit in the reservoir that I had not yet extracted." Billy further said, "I learned a valuable lesson that hard work and determination can take you to a level that exceeds an objective evaluation of your talents."

This attitude and approach to attainment enabled Billy to make history. And, by the way, it wasn't the last time he did so. Billy Payne went on to become chairman of Augusta National Golf Club (home of the Masters) and led the club to admit women members for the first time in its eighty-two year existence.

Are you similar to Billy Payne? Can your hard work and determination catapult your accomplishments to a level that exceeds your talents? In other words, are you doing not what you can, but what you can't?

Bill Porter

Even though he lived all his life in Portland, Oregon, this man merited a write-up in the obituary pages of the *Atlanta Journal-Constitution* when he died on December 3, 2013, at the age of eighty-one. Before his death, each workday of his adulthood started with the clanging clock. It's 5:45 a.m. He struggles to get up after another pain-filled night. It's difficult to dress because his fingers are a twisted gnarl. Because he can't drive, he catches a bus to work. It's mostly full of kids going to school.

He never got to do what these kids take for granted. No athletic activities. No skipping down the halls. No dates. No dances. When he was the age of these kids, he was placed in classes set aside for slow students (stupid, some said). But Bill wasn't stupid. He just had a body that did not respond to what his brain told it to do.

As soon as he was old enough to understand, his mother explained that his birth had been extremely difficult. The doctor had used an instrument that crushed a part of his brain. It caused cerebral palsy. He could hardly walk. His speech was garbled. The state considered him so handicapped that they designated him as unemployable and suggested disability payments. He refused.

It wasn't just the state that considered him unemployable. He applied for a job as a door-to-door salesman with Fuller Brush Company. They said he was incapable of carrying their samples with his handicapped hands. They also said he couldn't walk up and down sidewalk steps from house to house with his legs burdened by a bent-over body.

He applied for the same kind of work with J. R. Watkins Company, a household supply and materials manufacturer/distributor/seller somewhat similar to Fuller Brush Company. They, too, rejected Bill. However, he was relentless in his quest for a job. His persistent push for them to give him a chance motivated them to give Bill a sales territory. It was the worst territory in Portland—one where more than two or three predecessors had failed to perform. But Bill didn't mind one bit.

Here's a look at a typical day on Bill's sales beat.

Bill gets off the bus at his exit and heads straight for the local shoeshine shop, where they will tie his shoes for him each day. Because of major back surgery it is difficult for him to put on his shoes, much less tie the laces. He pays for a shoeshine at least twice a week because he knows he must look sharp when those knocked-on doors are opened to him. But not all of them are. To get enough doors to open and give him a chance to make a sale—make a living—he walks ten miles each and every day. It's a twelve-hour trek.

Those who don't know Bill and see him trudging through Portland neighborhoods wonder if he is drunk, or maybe blind. He stumbles along the level and flat sidewalks as if there are deep cracks, tree roots and potholes creating a not-so-smooth path to maneuver. Children laugh at his clumsy, clown-like gait. Yet, all his life, Bill made it on his own as a salesman. For years, he was the number-one salesperson in a four-state area of the northwest United States. He overcame and achieved so much that an Emmy-winning television movie was made of his life. He did what the social-service system said someone in his physical condition couldn't do. He did the best he can't!

In light of how these ordinary people excelled at the extraordinary and ended up doing what can't be done, are you and I ever justified in uttering any of the "can'ts" in the list below, which is repeated from the previous chapter?

I can't quit smoking. I can't swim. I can't remember names. I can't get a promotion. I can't keep a secret. I can't speak in front of an audience. I can't ride my bicycle a hundred miles each weekend. I can't cook. I can't jog a mile. I can't afford college. I can't find time to take my kids bowling. I can't start a business. I can't save 10 percent of my income. I can't build rapport with my neighbor. I can't balance my checkbook. I can't forgive him/her for_____. I can't learn a foreign language. I can't control my temper. I can't quit abusing alcohol. I can't get along with my in-laws. I can't save money. I can't grow flowers. I can't save my marriage. I can't apologize. I can't drive a stick shift. I can't tie a tie. I can't climb a mountain. I can't earn a living. I can't read one book a month. I can't control my children. I can't buy a house. I can't relax. I can't sew. I can't quit my job. I can't get over_____. I can't quit using foul language. I can't make all As and Bs. I can't lose weight. I can't take a chance on _____.

Shouldn't we do the best we can't?

CHAPTER 3

BE LIKE A TURTLE

That Doesn't Mean Slow

Have we gone soft? Do we have a backbone? Where is our courage? Are we a bunch of lily-livered chickens who've lost our pioneer passion? Those who left England to settle on our shores set sail knowing there might be stormy seas. Pirates were a possibility. They knew they could famish from a lack of food. They might die from deadly diseases. But the goal of coming to a land of opportunity, to America, was compelling enough that they fought through their fears and moved forward.

It didn't end there. After their landing at Plymouth Rock, the descendants of these early pioneers pushed to the Western Rockies. They forged rivers, cut through canyons, and staked out settlements in sometimes hostile lands. In the summers, they had to endure the blazing, blistering sun. In the winters, it was the bitter, blowing snow. Both could be deadly.

They cut through solid-rock mountains to lay tracks and build our railroads, then our roads, then our expressways. They gambled that heavier-than-air machines could actually fly and carry passengers. They beat smallpox, malaria, and polio. They overcame a dustbowl in the West and a depression across the nation. And they fought Hitler's monstrous military machine to keep us free. At the same time, they also battled and beat Mussolini of Italy and Hirohito of Japan.

As I write this chapter, I wonder where this display of daring and determined nerves of steel is as we face a pandemic called COVID-19. In a nationwide study, Matt Motta of Oklahoma State University found hesitancy, not heroics, in those surveyed regarding their willingness to take the preventive vaccine.

Most scientists, biologists, immunologists, and medical doctors agree that to conquer the coronavirus through herd immunity, a minimum of 75 percent of Americans need to take the shot. But Motta found we won't reach that level because 37 percent are afraid and unwilling to take a preventive shot. That's even though the vaccine was tested by over thirty thousand volunteers with less than one in a hundred of them suffering mild side effects of chill, fever, or fatigue for a day or two.

Speaking of chill, how did our society develop so many cold feet? Such faint hearts? Such weak knees? Such spinelessness? Such lack of guts? Such an absence of nerves? Where in the world is our bravery? Our pluck? Our grit? Our nerve? Our prowess? Our stoutness? Our spunk? Our spark? Our confidence? Our backbone? Our mettle? Our moxie? Our hardiness? Our adventurousness? Our audaciousness? Our resoluteness?

You see, the first step to doing the best you can't is to conjure up enough derring-do to will yourself to beat the odds and attempt the unusual or unlikely or uneasy. You have to exhibit a bold front. Take the bull by the horns. Walk through broken glass. Go through fire and water. Run the gauntlet. Take charge. Keep a stiff upper lip. Keep your chin up.

If you are going to do the best you can't, you must not be tied to the timid thousands. First, face your fear. Fight it. Move forward in spite of fear. You'll never achieve your goal if you are unwilling to "suck it up" and force yourself to try what you haven't tried. Or try again what did not work on your first, second, or third attempt. I learned these truths during my senior year in high school. I became aware of the importance of conjuring up enough courage to do what I really couldn't do.

Come with me now as I travel back in time to my senior year. I'm standing in front of the entire student body of Albert G. Parrish High. I'm scared. Not just scared—scared to death.

You see, most people would rather curl up in a cozy cuddle with a rattlesnake than give a public speech to their peers. That's what I was about to force myself to do. Not the rattlesnake bit (pun intended). I was about to give a speech. Back then, I had a hard enough time ordering a burger and fries at the Tastee Freeze, let alone addressing a crowd of clamorous, catcalling classmates. I had no business being up there. So what was I doing there?

Well, I was tired of feeling inferior. I was tired of feeling insecure. I was tired of being overlooked, staying in the background, always following, never leading, so scared.

As a kid growing up in Selma, Alabama, I didn't have a dad. He left when I was one year old. My mom didn't have an education. She supported four kids on the minimum wages she earned all her life. She could not afford to send me to school wearing the latest new stylish clothes my classmates wore. Momma didn't own a car, so I couldn't date. You can't pick 'em up on a bicycle. Most of the time, I felt I couldn't match up to my classmates. The only thing not inferior about me was my inferiority complex. It was super superior. I was infinitely insecure.

Being tired of second-class status, I decided I wanted to be at least somewhat similar to those who led our school's social set. So I aspired to do something big and important. I wanted to be on the student council. Maybe I wouldn't feel like such a nobody if I was elected to the student council.

That required a speech. I had to summon up enough pioneering spirit to risk humiliation, embarrassment, defeat.

I practiced. I prepared. I delivered a dignified Gettysburg-worthy address to my bathroom mirror. And when the time finally came to rise to the microphone, I took a deep breath and I began to speak.

That's when I realized something I had never known before. I was fluent in five languages. English, of course. The other four were stuttering, stammering, stumbling, and spitting. Oh, it was bad. I couldn't stay behind the podium. I was so stressed and nervous that I paced back and forth like a chicken with its head cut off.

I planned to tell a joke to loosen up the audience, make myself likeable, and thereby gain rapport and win over my classmates. Yep, the audience started laughing. But they weren't laughing *with* me. They were laughing *at* me. And they kept laughing.

All in all, it was awful. An awful speech. An awful experience.

Worst of all, once I stumbled off the stage, I realized my election chances were a long shot at best.

But then … there have been longer shots. For example, Tom Dempsey. My stammering speech was a few years ahead of him, but if seventeen-year-old me could have peered into the future, I probably would have taken comfort in the legend of the New Orleans Saints kicker. It's a legend still told to this day across the bayous of Baton Rouge to Bossier City and beyond.

The day was November 8, 1970. The place was Tulane Stadium. This was years before the Super Dome. The playoff-bound Detroit Lions looked to be on their way to certain victory when they iced a chip-shot field goal to go ahead 17–16 with eleven seconds left over what was a woeful one-win Saints team.

Saints quarterback Billy Kilmer needed a real Hail Mary pass just to get close to reasonable field-goal range. It didn't happen. After one pitiful play, the Saints found themselves with two seconds left and well on the farther-away-from-the-goalpost side of the fifty-yard line. At the time, field goals were almost never attempted from the opponent's side of the fifty-yard line even though the goalposts were then on the goal line rather than ten yards farther back as they are today. On the rare occasions when they were tried, they were woefully off target. But what did the Saints have to lose?

But what about their kicker, Dempsey? He faced losing face. Attempting to kick a football so far was foolish futility. Staring him in the face was certain failure in front of a full stadium and a television audience of millions.

They called upon their kicker anyhow. They asked Tom Dempsey to kick an impossible, never-before-seen sixty-three-yard field goal. What a preposterous proposition. But it would be even more preposterous coming off the foot of Tom Dempsey, a man who was born with no toes on his kicking foot.

That's right. Tom Dempsey had a club foot. He couldn't even wear a regular football-kicking shoe. Instead, he wore a specially made flat-toed shoe that ended where his toes weren't. He had no business being on the football field. His entire NFL career was impossible. But long before his NFL career, Dempsey dared to make the impossible his business.

From childhood, he'd been told what he couldn't do. He didn't listen. He didn't withdraw and hide when neighborhood children laughed at his somewhat hobbled walk. He didn't sulk when he was the last one chosen for the softball or football games his Little League friends and acquaintances wanted to play. He didn't give up when his handicap made him mess up.

I never met Tom Dempsey, but I like to think he knew something that I came to find out when I was in front of the auditorium audience and behind that podium at Albert G. Parrish High. In order to do the best you can't—indeed, in order to achieve greatness—you have to "be like a turtle." I don't mean slow. I mean you have to stick your neck out. It's the only way the turtle gets anywhere.

If a turtle is born on a side of the road where the pond he first enjoyed is drying up, green grass is dying, and no juicy bugs remain, he needs to cross that road to a bigger, better pond. There's a chance the turtle gets run over, sure. But most of the time, he gets to the other side.

If we're ever going to get anywhere, we have to stick our neck out. We have to take a chance. We have to conjure up the courage to change. And change is contrary to our nature. We are creatures of habit. If you don't believe that, I'll wager you get up on the same side of the bed every day. And I'll bet you tie the same shoe first each time you lace up.

Sticking your neck out can be scary. It's much easier and safer to stay put in our shells. On the other hand, the sunlight is shut out of that shell. It's boring in that shell. Dreams don't come true in that shell. And the ball doesn't fly sixty-three yards in that shell.

But that day in Tulane Stadium, it did just that. It went even farther.

In a call that has gone down in New Orleans Saints history, a bored-sounding CBS sportscaster, Don Criqui, appeared to be wrapping up another predictable loss for the Saints. "He's trying a sixty-three-yard field goal," Criqui said with zero excitement. "[If] Tom Dempsey hits this one, he's got a very slight wind at his back, he'll set a National Football League record in addition to winning the game."

Then the kick. The flat-toed shoe connecting with the pigskin. The football flipping end over end. The ball traveling farther and straighter than anyone in the stadium could have believed possible.

Criqui's tone changed. "I don't believe this!" he blurted. "It's good! I don't believe it! The field-goal attempt was good from sixty-three yards away! It's incredible!"

Tulane Stadium went wild. Tom Dempsey was mobbed by his joyous teammates. And he danced in his flat-toed shoe that day.

That flat-toed shoe is now on display in the NFL Hall of Fame in Canton, Ohio. His record stood for nearly forty years. All because he chose to be like a turtle. He stuck his neck out.

As for me, well, I'm no Tom Dempsey. But somehow, someway, I also made the goal. I won the student council election that year. It would never have happened if I had not stuck my neck out and risked rejection at the hands of my classmates.

Maybe they voted for me because they felt sympathy for such a sorry speechmaker. Maybe they chose to be kindhearted and lift up a fellow who was down on himself. Maybe they weren't impressed with the speech but were impressed with the gall I showed by trying. Whatever the reason, I would never have even had a chance at their votes if I had not done what I could not do. I did the best I can't.

And now, after a lifetime in politics and business, people are crazy enough to pay me to speak. Me. A motivational speaker who has

been in front of civic clubs, conventions, universities, churches, cor-
porations, sales teams, training enclaves, and business groups in over
half our nation's states. Me. A man fluent in stuttering, stammering,
stumbling, and spitting.

Perhaps a more significant time I stuck my neck out was just a few
months after that speech. It was the summer after I was a high school
senior giving that stuttering, stammering speech. I was back on the
job I'd had each of the two summers prior to my graduation. Thank
God my buddy Bo lost his pants at that time. Let me explain.

Bo Morrow was an acquaintance of mine because we went to the
same church. Even though we were not best friends, for some reason,
Bo ended up taking me to a place I never intended to go. A place I'd
never dreamed in my wildest imagination that I would ever wind up.
College.

I had been spending summer months laying tar and gravel on flat roofs
in Selma, Alabama. Yeah, with hundred-degree sun over my head and
150-degree tar under my feet, that job was as fun as it sounds.

One day, Bo mentioned he was headed to his alma mater to pick up
some clothes he had left in his dorm closet. He asked if I wanted to
ride along. It seemed like a nice break from the multimillion-degree
heat, so I hopped in his car and we headed north toward Nashville.
Little did I realize we weren't just driving toward Bo's laundry. We
were driving toward my future.

When we rolled onto that beautiful green campus of Lipscomb
University, I really couldn't believe it. I was mesmerized by its mag-
nificence. Its stately buildings, manicured lawns, tremendously tall
trees, and winding walkways presented another world I'd never pic-
tured. Peaceful. Placid. Perfect. Pretty much the exact opposite of a
hot-tarred roof in Selma.

So while Bo went to get his pants and things, I walked directly into the administration building, stepped up to the front desk, and said, "I'd like to enroll in your college." Kind of in the same way you might order a chili-dog with all the fixins at DQ, I ordered an education. It usually doesn't work like that, but I was naïve, inexperienced, and unsophisticated and did not know that at the time. I was sorta starting to stick my neck out again, like I had a few months earlier with that speech.

Now, the lady at the front desk could have laughed me out of the building. If she had, that might have sent me scurrying straight back to my safe shell in Selma.

She didn't laugh. "What made you choose Lipscomb?" she asked spritely, as if new students wandered in from Alabama every day. Um. Well. Uh. Now that was an appropriate question, but I'm sure I did not give an appropriate answer.

"I just rode up here with my friend and saw your campus," I said. "And I think it is a beautiful place." At the same time, I'm also thinking it's also a place a poor, unprepared, insecure kid from Alabama had no place being. After all, nobody in my family went to college. College was for other people. Plus, I was what you would call "college challenged."

My high school grades were low school grades. I could not read well because I had difficulty concentrating. My mind did not easily focus on a book's page, thus, it wandered afar. I had ADHD before it was called that.

By the way, ADHD made some of my college courses doubly difficult because many required more than listening to lectures. They required reading. Studying. That was especially true of kinesiology. I did so poorly at kinesiology that I still can't tell you exactly what it is. More than once, I thought about dropping out and getting a full-time job. Then again, I didn't want to go back into that dark shell.

But back to the lady in the administration building. "Well, how do you plan on paying for your education?" she asked, even more spritely this time. "I have no idea," I said. "How much does it cost?"

I don't remember the price, but I assure you, it was more than I had on me at the time. After telling me the university would help me find a job so I could pay my tuition, room, and board, she handed me a bunch of papers and applications to fill out. With each hastily, haphazardly scribbled form I completed, I was coming farther and farther out of my shell.

There was a risk I couldn't earn enough to buy books. I might not pass exams. I might even get homesick for Selma. It was scary. However, when I strode off that stage in my cap and gown four years later, I knew I was like the turtle. I had stuck my neck out, and it got me someplace.

By the way, that was the one and probably only time I also wanted to be slow like the turtle. I liked being on that stage holding up my diploma for my poor old uneducated momma to see. She was pretty proud, as was I. So there was no scurrying off the stage to get back to my seat. Stand on stage. Soak in the glory.

Getting ahead—doing the best you can't—also awaits you if you convince yourself that sticking your neck out is better than staying stuck in the status quo. Just as I had no business giving that speech and attending that university, and just as Tom Dempsey had no business being on that football field, there is something you have no business doing and somewhere you have no business being. Make that your business. Be like a turtle. Stick your neck out.

Oh, if you're afraid you'll fail, read on and you'll see that even if you do fail, it does not deem you doomed.

CHAPTER 4

WALK THE PLANK

Conceive; Believe; Achieve

Here's a $100 bill. I want you to have it. (I know, this is a book. But just play along.)

I will pay you this clean, crisp C-note if, without tripping and falling, you walk this straight, steady, simple hundred-foot board that I have laid on this smooth, solid, flat floor. We got a deal?

Some of you readers are probably smart-mouthed show-offs. I can hear you holler, "Bud, for $100, I'll walk the plank backward." Hey, I like your spunk. But wait. I've got a better deal for you. More money. A lot more money. A million dollars more. It's all yours, and all you have to do is walk that same straight, steady, simple wooden board. Only this time, it's across the deepest chasm of the Grand Canyon. No ropes. No handrails. No nets. No nothing, just like with the plank on the flat floor. Now, though, that same wooden board is one thousand feet above the raging Colorado River.

Still interested? Now are there any smart-mouthed show-offs hankering to holler how you'll walk the plank backward? No. Well, what's the difference? One major difference is that you *think you can* walk the plank when it is on the solid flat floor. You *don't think you can* walk it across the Grand Canyon.

That brings us to the next step in doing the best you can't. You're the turtle in the previous chapter. You've stuck your neck out. But that's just the beginning. The turtle still has to cross the road. He won't do it if he is too awfully afraid of automobiles. He won't do it if he feels it's likely he will get run over. Oh, he is a realist. He understands there is at least a chance he will get run over. But he'll cross the road if he believes there is a better chance he will end up on the other side where there is more water and juicier bugs than where he now is. His positive outlook must be stronger than his negative outlook. He needs at least some degree of confidence that he will make it.

History is full of people who have been confronted with choices similar to the one I offered you, to walk the plank for $100 or $1,000,000. Stay on solid ground or step out to what's not so sure. Not so safe.

In the case of Nik Wallenda, that's no mere metaphor. On June 24, 2013, the twenty-four-year-old stepped off the Arizona dirt onto a two-inch-thick steel cable some 1,500 feet above the Little Colorado River on the Navajo Nation near the Grand Canyon. No ropes. No nets. No nothings. It was a breezy day in northeastern Arizona, and the world was watching, along with a camera crew from the Discovery Channel.

The fifth-generation member of the famous Flying Wallendas probably would have scoffed at our solid, stable, simple wooden plank, while most of us would take one step onto his rigid rope and plummet to the ground like Wil. E. Coyote. But Nik Wallenda sauntered on that high wire as though he was taking a Sunday stroll. That is, until the winds came.

It was during the thirteenth minute of that twenty-two-minute walk that a stiff breeze came in off the canyons. Nik Wallenda stopped in his towering tracks. He teetered. He tottered. He crouched on the rope as it swayed back and forth. Like I said, he had no harness or other help. It was just him and the rope. Well, he did have paramedics waiting and watching a little more than 1,500 feet below. But what could they do if Nik took a step and slipped? Chances are, the coroner would have been the more appropriate emergency responder.

That's the danger of walking the plank. If you are attempting to do the best you can't, at some point in the process, a breeze blows, a wild wind will come rushing in, and you'll find yourself teetering and tottering. Your wind may be the fear of failing financially. The fear you won't gain ground. The fear of being embarrassed. The fear of being laughed at, scoffed at by those who are watching from the edge of the canyon. One thing's for sure: there is no net when you choose to walk the plank—when you choose to do the best you can't.

As for our buddy Nik Wallenda, it turns out he didn't need a net. As the cable bounced in that breeze, he kept his cool, he kept his calm and, most importantly, he kept his balance. And when the wind died down, he slowly moved on. But before he did, he muttered a prayer that was captured by the Discovery Channel microphones. "Thank you, Lord," he said. "Thank you for calming that cable." Nine minutes later, he was back on solid soil, tall and triumphant.

Thankfully, for his fabulous feat, I didn't offer Nik the million dollars that I offered you, dear reader. It would have definitely depleted my deposits. In fact, I don't know what Discovery Channel or anyone else paid him, but I bet the view alone was worth a million. Maybe more.

That observation raises the question: after sticking your neck out, what's the next key to your, figuratively speaking, gaining a million-dollar view? To walking the plank? To doing the best you can't?

It's somewhat simple. It boils down to your attitude. Attitude determines altitude. Confidence will cause you to cross the canyon. Concern will cause you to stay safely on the side. I sometimes say it another way. If you think you can, you can. If you think you can't, you're right. When the plank was on a smooth, solid, flat floor, your attitude was, "I can." When the same plank was across the Grand Canyon, your attitude was, "I can't."

You've heard it said that a chain is no stronger than its weakest link. Well, the brain is no stronger than its weakest think. If you don't believe that, then before you read another word, try this smile/frown test right now. I guarantee you will smile rather than frown if you will envision a beautiful rainbow in your mind's eye. Go ahead; think about a colorful rainbow and you'll see you smile as a result. Or recall your favorite song or funniest joke and, again, you will smile, not frown. Now, think about drinking pure lemon juice and swirling it around in your mouth. Or think about sliding down a banister that turns into a razor blade halfway down its length. It is impossible to smile as you did when thinking about the rainbow, song, and joke. You cannot help but frown, maybe even cringe as you conjure up the lemon juice and razor blade. This shows that you must control your thoughts, for they control your outlook—control whether you smile or frown. Your thoughts, in the final analysis, control how you act and react.

An illustration I have used many times is a common-sense example of the power of our thoughts and attitude. A family relocated and, upon meeting their new neighbor, asked what kind of neighborhood they had moved into. The neighbor said he'd be happy to answer their question but first wanted to know what kind of neighborhood they had just left.

The answer was that they had relocated because their old neighborhood was so horrible. The neighbors were not very friendly. They stuck their nose where it didn't belong. Their kids were loud. Their dogs barked continuously and growled menacingly. The cats messed up the flower beds. Lawns were not very well maintained. Everybody's property was unkempt.

After hearing the relocated family's response to his question about the neighborhood they had just left, the fellow to whom the question was asked offered no encouragement in his reply. He told them he was sorry to say, but they were going to find their new neighborhood to be pretty much like the one they had left. Families did not interact in positive ways. Kids were constantly creating a commotion. Dogs were a menace. Cats dug around bulbs and broke fragile flowers. Yards needed weeding much better than they were and needed mowing much more frequently. And there were a lot of fences that needed missing pickets replaced, along with some houses that could use a fresh paint job.

Another family relocated to the same neighborhood just a couple of days later and asked the same person the same question that had previously been asked. He again responded that he would be happy to answer their question but would like to first know what kind of neighborhood they had just relocated from. The answer was that they were sincerely sad that their work had made it necessary to relocate because their old neighborhood was like heaven on earth. Families regularly got together for cookouts. They helped one another solve problems. The pets were so cuddly and friendly, and the kids happily played together. Yards were beautiful and people took pride in keeping their houses in good repair.

After hearing this reply to his question, his response to the new family was that they were mighty lucky because they had relocated to the exact kind of neighborhood they had left. They would find friendly folks. Kids even went door to door to serenade seniors who resided there. Suppers were shared once a month. People were positive. There were no problem pets. Lawns were manicured, and there were such constant improvements to property that homes seemed to always look brand-new.

Since the person who was questioned about the quality of the neighborhood gave two totally different answers to the same question, was he dishonest? Could two contradictory answers both be honest and accurate? Maybe that question is well answered in the Bible, where it says, "For as he thinks in his heart, so is he." (Proverbs 23:7, KJV) That being the case, it is not only possible, but likely that the same neighborhood is seen in a positive light by a person with a good attitude and is seen in a negative light by a person with a bad attitude. One's viewpoint may well determine whether one has a million-dollar view.

Therefore, while it's possible that you'll fall when attempting to walk the plank across whatever canyon you are confronting, you have to conjure up enough confidence to believe that with the right preparation and planning, you won't plummet. While it's scary, not totally safe, and there are no guarantees, you must not dwell on defeat. Instead, like the train in the children's book, *The Little Engine that Could*, your thoughts must be, "I think I can. I think I can. I think I can." It's this spirit that will instill in you the determination to do the daunting. Maybe even the daring. It's a proven principle; you can achieve what you conceive if you believe.

Your will is even strong enough to negate the pain that normally follows your worries and wounds. My dentist tells me I'm one of the best people he knows at preventing pain without popping pills. When I first started going to Dr. Steve Carter, he wanted to write a prescription for me to take when whatever painkilling shot he had given me had worn off after he performed a major procedure like a root canal or extraction of a wisdom tooth. I would always tell him not to waste his pen and prescription pad, as I did not want to ingest any more drugs into my body than absolutely necessary. I explained that I could pretend or imagine I felt good and had no soreness or discomfort and that such positive thinking would prevent pain. Thankfully, these thoughts turned out to be true.

According to Dr. Fredrick Kalz, merely thinking that something can cause a cure can do so even though there are no scientific, biological, epidemiological, or medical reasons for a cure to take place. Writing in the *Canadian Medical Association Journal*, he noted that almost all cultures around the world have mythical, almost magical, means to curing aches, pains, sicknesses, and diseases. He further wrote that they *all work* if a person believes strongly enough in them. Belief brings relief!

When I was growing up, I had some warts on the back of my hand. They were unsightly. Ugly. The possibility that someone might notice them embarrassed me. I was certain no girl would want to hold my hand. Momma could not afford to take me to a doctor to rid me of what she saw as a minor distraction, not a major disease. Thus, in desperation, I decided to try a "voodoo remedy" I heard about from one of my friend's somewhat senile, certainly strange, self-proclaimed soothsaying great-grandmother.

She said warts could be cured by cutting a sweet potato in half, rubbing one of the cut sides of the potato across the warts for six strokes, planting it under a dripping faucet on the south side of the house, and then doing the same thing with the other half of the potato and planting it under a dripping faucet on the north side of the house. Probably because I didn't really believe it would work, my warts didn't disappear. However, there was one benefit to the ritual. After practicing the procedure over and over again, I grew an enormous crop of sweet potatoes.

In his 1952 best-selling book, *The Power of Positive Thinking*, Norman Vincent Peale told readers: "Expect great things and great things will come." He promulgated the idea that positive thinking is ideal, even if the end results don't totally and exactly measure up to your thoughts, wishes, and goals. An example of that is the saying that if you shoot for the moon and fail to make it, you'll still land among the stars. Perhaps that turned out to be the case in my war with warts. I didn't make them go away, but I had a super supply of succulent sweet potatoes for supper.

In the movie *The Secret: Dare to Dream* starring Katie Holmes, and streaming on Amazon at the time of this writing, there is a line that says, "The more you think about something, the more you draw it to you." That line mirrors what I earlier in this book quoted from Proverbs 23:7 (KJV). It is worth repeating: "For as he thinks in his heart, so is he."

Whether he realized it or not, internationally acclaimed soccer superstar Cristiano Ronaldo parroted this philosophy propounded by Proverbs when he signed a new multiyear, multimillion-dollar contract at the age of thirty-six. That's an age when most soccer players are worn out from constant travel, eons of extensive exercise, and innumerable injuries. They are ready for retirement. When the press questioned him about his "old" age, Ronaldo said, "It doesn't matter the age; it's the mind."

Franklin Delano Roosevelt, the only president America has ever had to serve more than two terms, emphasized the importance of thoughts when he said, "The only limit to our realization of tomorrow will be our doubts of today." Even though the paralysis of polio forced Roosevelt into a wheelchair before he ever campaigned for and was elected president, he never let negative notions or debilitating doubts limit or take a toll on his tomorrow.

This principle of positive thinking has been referred to by some as the Law of Attraction—a belief that your experiences have a direct correlation to your thoughts. Thus, to walk the plank, you must believe that walk really is a possibility in your life. You have to see yourself actually doing it. Maybe be like the little boy whose favorite sweet treat was marshmallows. He constantly craved and consumed them. One night, he dreamed he ate a fifty-pound marshmallow. The next morning, he woke up and his foam rubber pillow was gone.

Now, the kind of belief that I'm suggesting is essential to walking the plank, essential to sailing west to get east, essential to stuffing mailboxes with your feet, essential to making the winning bid for the Olympics, essential to being the number-one salesperson even though the state says you are so disabled you should be on their disability welfare rolls, essential to whatever your "can't" happens to be, is much more than a dream. This belief is much more than wishful thinking.

In later chapters, you will see examples of belief that are much more than wishful thinking, and I'll describe the kind of belief that is essential to doing the best you can't. For now, though, I want to end this chapter by telling you about a major "can't" I achieved right after my graduation from Lipscomb University. Figuratively speaking, this "can't" was a walk across the Grand Canyon on the plank with which I earlier challenged you. This was a marshmallow much more than the fifty-pounder in the boy's dream. It was making the winning bid on both the Summer and Winter Olympics for the same city for the same year. It was running a three-minute mile. It began because of belief. Indeed, if I had not believed from the very beginning that it was possible, there would have been no beginning. Thus, positive thinking right before college graduation made it possible to transcribe these thoughts and have this tale to tell.

(Please keep in mind, I don't share any of my personal experiences or achievements to be a boastful braggart. I earlier wrote about a turtle. Let me tell you something else about a turtle. If he is on top of a fence post, he did not get there by himself. Therefore, I am aware that anything of significance I may have accomplished in my life is largely because someone—many someones—helped me. At the very least, they showed me the principles, processes, and procedures I needed to follow if I was ever going to do the best I can't. In turn, I am sharing these principles, processes, and procedures with you by way of this book. In doing so, my hope is you will conclude that if this old boy who grew up socially and economically disadvantaged, and who is not tremendously talented, could do what realistically couldn't be done, then you, too, can do what you can't. I'm hopeful my example will both educate and motivate you to make a major mark in business, athletics, education, politics, medicine, farming, science, family life, community life, personal life, whatever. I'm hopeful it will help you become the person you wish you could be, not the person you feel you are doomed to be.)

The story I'm sharing involves an impossibility that I did not know was impossible. I was only twenty-one, so I sure did not have the maturity to do it. I did not have enough training to do it. I did not have the knowledge to do it. I did not have the money to do it. I certainly did not have the experience to do it. I did not even know who to ask to help me do it. Maybe I did it mainly because I didn't know I couldn't do it. I didn't know enough to have troubling thoughts. Thus, no debilitating doubts could deter me.

There is a saying most of us have heard or spoken: "Ignorance is bliss." Maybe I was too ignorant to know what I didn't know. Too ignorant to know I couldn't do it. All I knew was that there was public speaking and fundraising involved.

My stuttering, stammering, stumbling, and spitting during my first speech back at Albert G. Parrish High School motivated me to minor in speech at Lipscomb. On top of my improvement at public speaking, one of the part-time jobs I found to work my way through college was making phone calls at night to Nashville residents to raise money for a local charity. This was years before the advent of cell phones, and most people would answer their landline home phones and actually converse with callers. Feeling somewhat competent in those two components—public speaking and asking for donations—gave me enough confidence to blissfully believe I could do what I was about to attempt.

Maybe a subtitle for what I'm going to share with you could aptly be named "From Nashville to New York." Or "From Tampa to Toronto." Stay tuned for the explanation.

It was just a few weeks before I would receive my bachelor's degree on that stage in Nashville. Dr. Ira North asked me to come to his office to discuss a job opportunity for which he had been asked to refer someone. In his mind, I was that someone.

Because of his dynamism, energy, and enthusiasm, students called Dr. Ira North "Firey Irey." He knew me because I was in one of his speech classes. Firey Irey told me he had recommended me for a job opportunity. It was in New York City, thus the subtitle "From Nashville to New York." The opportunity's outstanding outcome was written about in over four hundred newspapers across the United States and Canada. One of those newspapers was *The Tampa Times* and another was *The Toronto Star*, thus the subtitle "From Tampa to Toronto."

My figurative walk across the Grand Canyon involved a challenge created by a church. Not a megachurch. It was a mini-church with only sixty-six members. They met in a little building less than three miles from where the 1964–65 World's Fair would be located. They wanted someone to preach from their pulpit each Sunday and during the rest of the week work on establishing an exhibit at the World's Fair. The little church was called the Queens Church of Christ because it was in the Queens Borough of New York City.

Firey Irey knew I could give a speech because I had done it in his class. He knew I had fundraising experience from my part-time evening job making phone calls for a local charity. He knew I possessed at least some knowledge of the Bible because Lipscomb University was a Christian college that required all students to take a daily Bible class, no matter their major. He told the little church, "Bud's your man." Like, this Bud's *really* for you!

Also, this Bud was really for them because I was cheap. They actually needed three people: a minister, a professional fundraiser, and someone who could staff and manage an exhibit that would attract over a hundred thousand people from all over the world. They got three for the price of one at the $400 per month salary they told Firey Irey was all they could afford.

I'll always be grateful to my then wife, who I married just before starting my senior year at Lipscomb, because she got a job at the telephone company to pay for our rent and food and my college tuition during our last year in Nashville. She deserves tons of respect and appreciation for putting her education on pause so I could acquire mine. And she never complained about it. In New York, however, she did not work outside the home, so we lived on little. Hey, New York City ain't cheap, so living on $400 a month is not easy. But walking around staring in amazement at skyscrapers was entertaining to this small-town Southern soul—and it was free!

Churches of Christ exist all over the world, but they don't have a world headquarters. Each congregation is autonomous. Whatever project is pursued by a congregation needs no approval from a centralized authority. There is none. There is no mega-mission or broad-based board to assist with advice, financing, or other kinds of support when a congregation constructs a building, sends missionaries abroad, hires ministers, or envisions other endeavors. Or when it decides to have an exhibit at the World's Fair. Other congregations can choose to help with a sister congregation's cause or challenge. If they do not want to support a specific one, such as the World's Fair exhibit, then the dream dies.

My major was physical education. I was planning to be a coach. My mom, limited by her ninth-grade education and narrow world view, never told me I could study to be an investment banker. Neither of us even knew what that was. She didn't tell me I could study to be an engineer, a scientist, a mortgage broker, a merchandiser, a marketer, an actuary (what was that?), an astronaut, or a chemist. I did not have the vision to see beyond the little world I had thus far experienced. But having played football, baseball, and basketball in high school, I knew what coaching was. Thus, a coaching career was my clear choice.

So how does a fellow with a physical education degree qualify to fill a pulpit? Most religious groups would say, "He can't." However, in Churches of Christ, there is no clerical certification or license needed to preach. No ecclesiastical exams for entry. No seminary studies stipulated. No ordination rigors required for a religious role. Thus, this wet-behind-the-ears kid from a Southern town with a population of less than twenty thousand, who is slightly improved from his days of stuttering, stammering, stumbling, and spitting, and who has raised, over many months, maybe $10,000 by phone, takes off for the city of ten million to raise ... well, I'll impart that information by quoting from one of those four hundred newspapers that thought our outcome was so outstanding.

First, a couple of story headlines. The April 4, 1964, *Tampa Times* headline read, "Tiny Church Didn't Know Defeat." The April 18, 1964, edition of the *Edmonton Journal* (Edmonton, Alberta, Canada) proclaimed, "Fair Miracle: Congregation of 66 Wouldn't Say Can't."

> Then, these words from the April 18, 1964, *Edmonton Journal*: "The little Queens church is a small little church. It has gone virtually unrecognized for years and would continue to do so perhaps except for one startling development. This little band of Christians will spend over $400,000 for a major exhibit at the 1964-65 New York World's Fair ... The little Queens church numbers only 66. Sixty-six members on its rolls and one would think right off that surely this must be a group of very wealthy church members, perhaps all millionaires. Quite to the contrary, the average annual income of this dedicated little group is less than $6,000 per family. The story of how this 66 had the vision, the tenacity, the dogged determination and the outright gall to attempt such an ambitious undertaking simply defies the imagination."

"Along Side Giants"

"Yet on April 22, 1964, when the Great Fair opens,
there the little Queens church will be with its magnificent exhibit alongside the major protestant denominations of America. Few of the Protestant
groups will have a more costly display at the Fair
and the little group will have more space than 11 of
the 14 exhibitors and as much as the other three in
the Protestant and Orthodox Center. Let Lawrence
(Bud) Stumbaugh, youthful minister of the church
and a native Alabaman, tell the story ... 'Since our
church building is located near the World's Fair site,
we began to hear talk around the neighborhood of the
proposed religious pavilion. We thought we would
simply inquire as to what exhibit space rented for. We
must admit when we learned that the price was $75
per square foot, we were a little taken back.'

"Huge Problem"

'As we surveyed the situation and decided on the
amount of space we would want, we found the rental
alone would come to $60,000. This, of course, did
not take into consideration a few hundred thousand
dollars more for construction of the exhibit, stocking
it with brochures, films and tracts, hiring of personnel
to man the space, and any number of expenditures
that we could not at that time foresee. Bank balance of
the Queens Church of Christ at the time showed less
than $200. However, we had a total of some $3,000
in our church building fund which had gathered over
quite a long period. We would have to have $7,000

for the down payment on the exhibit space and by the time we spoke to the Fair, most of the space had already been taken, another religious group had an option on the space we wanted and time was running out. We had to work against the clock.'

The article continued thusly. "Bud Stumbaugh hit the road to speak to sister churches to see if they would help him raise the remaining $4,000 after the little church drew out its life savings and applied $3,000 on the project. Although the members in the Churches of Christ in America number some 2,000,000 and there are more than 15,000 congregations, there is no national headquarters, no earthly head, indeed, no one in greater authority than the leaders, usually the elders, of a local congregation. So Stumbaugh had no national treasury to go to for his $4,000—much less his $400,000. He traveled to the South, an area he knew well, and spoke nightly at Churches of Christ in Alabama and Tennessee. Little by little the funds came dribbling in. Then the program went into gear. The Queens church very boldly wrote to 74 ministers, advertising and public relations executives, film producers, designers and other business executives, members of sister congregations in 20 states and asked for these men at their expense to come to New York to discuss how this great project could be carried out with a high degree of quality."

"56 Attended"

"Stumbaugh said, 'We were quite overwhelmed when 56 left busy schedules to attend a special meeting here in April, 1963. Many others either phoned or wired regrets. The first reaction of most of these church leaders was one of doubt that the big effort could succeed. But without a single exception these leaders caught the vision and as one man said it must be done.'"

Continuing from the latter part of the *Edmonton Journal*: "So on Sunday, April 26, the little church will realize a great ambition and have its regular morning worship service in the great World's Fair. They'll have an old-fashioned church service in the gigantic Fair Pavilion Auditorium and the millions who pass by will not know of the hardship and struggles the little church went through to get there. In addition, millions of radio listeners will hear the church service broadcast on two major radio networks, the Mutual Broadcasting System and the American Broadcasting Company. The little church never knew it couldn't be done."

Imagine, millions of radio listeners made possible by a mere sixty-six dedicated people, plus one recent college grad who didn't know he couldn't raise $400,000. By the way, $400,000 in 1964 is equivalent to $3,371,831.72 in 2022.

On top of the fundraising feat, our exhibit drew more personal visitors than any other religious exhibitor in the pavilion we occupied. That included the Billy Graham Association as well as Baptist, Methodist, Lutheran, Presbyterian, Episcopal, and other religious groups that were far better known "household names" and that had national and international boards to bolster them, financially and otherwise. (In a later chapter, I'll share with you one of the main features that attracted so many people to our exhibit. The really interesting part of that feature was that it was borne out of a mistake I made.)

The lesson that, hopefully, will be learned from the above is that you shouldn't make the mistake of thinking negatively, thinking too small, and thinking there are things you can't do. Happiness and happenings are a matter of mind over matter. Your attitude will determine your altitude: whether you soar like an airplane or sink like an anchor. It bears repeating. If you think you can, you can. If you think you can't, you're right. Yes, you can achieve what your mind can conceive, if you believe. Walking the plank is possible, but only if you think it is.

CHAPTER 5

FAILURE IS SELDOM FATAL

But Fearing Failure Is Fatal

Right after birth, you failed the basics—bladder and bowel control. For a year or so, it was not comfortable, perhaps even chafing, for you. Nor was it convenient for your parents. However, it didn't kill you or them. Your failure was not fatal. Thanks to potty training, neither was your failure forever.

After a few months, another babyhood basic began in frustrating failure. You may even have experienced bruises and broken bones from the falls you endured while failing at this basic. But failure at your first efforts to walk would have been fatal and forever only if you were so scared to stand after each stumble that you never stood back up.

Back when I was growing up, we had so few restrictions and broke so many "stay safe rules and regulations" set by today's society that it's a wonder how anyone from my generation fell, literally and figuratively speaking, got back up, and lived to tell about it. We were born to moms who smoked throughout pregnancy. A few even drank alcohol. We were laid on our tummies in bassinets and cribs coated—contaminated—in lead-based colors. There were no child-proof lids on the jars we could so easily open. No baby booster seats for the cars in which we rode. No seat belts either. We even rode in the back of pickup trucks, sometimes standing. We also rode our bikes without helmets, as stores did not carry them. On the personal side, when I was in college, I hitchhiked rides from strangers as I went back and forth from Selma to Nashville. Hitchhiking was fairly common by kids both older and younger than I.

Other potential failures we faced might even be described as dangers. We'd leave home early in the morning to play with our friends until just before dark, and there were no cell phones to check if everything was alright. At eight or nine years old, we got our first BB guns, yet failed to fulfill the dire prophecies about shooting out someone's eye. We ate Moon Pies and Twinkies and washed them down with Kool-Aid sweetened with heaping helpings of sugar. We even ate mud pies made from real dirt. Our mud pies were also loaded with sugar, and sometimes there was a worm or two in them. We played baseball in neighbors' empty lots that were punctuated with potholes and riddled with rocks. Occasionally, that led to twisted ankles and balls that bounced in unexpected directions for destinations like front teeth. And Little Leaguers played with wooden bats because aluminum ones had not been invented. We took our chances that a bat could break and impale us with its splinters. On top of that, we faced Little League tryouts where not everyone made the team.

What'd we do about it? We just dealt with the disappointment. Then we practiced in hopes of getting better. We certainly did not sue the league for being discriminatory or unfair. Talk about lawsuits. I can't remember any neighbor ever being sued as a result of the injuries incurred on their property either. Hey, you climb your neighbors' trees and take your chances on breaking a branch, falling, and suffering a bruise or broken bone. It was not the next-door family's fault.

None of the above is a meant to diminish the importance of safe and healthy lifestyles. Mothers should certainly not smoke or drink while pregnant. I don't recommend smoking or drinking for women who are not pregnant either. In fact, I don't recommend it for women or men. Ever. It's powerfully positive to practice health and safety measures that modern research and discoveries have shown us can add years to our life. I just don't want us to be so averse to any risk or danger, real or perceived, that we can't add life to our years. What fun is it to live long if we don't love living? A life full of years does not equate to years full of life. That's especially true if those years are empty of adventure, excitement, exceeding limits, overcoming obstacles, conquering challenges, and doing the best we can't.

Earlier in this book, I challenged you to walk a plank across the Grand Canyon. Now, failing at that would be fatal. Attempting to jump off the Empire State Building without a parachute would be fatal. Cuddling a cobra would be fatal. Except for these kinds of extremes which sane people rarely even contemplate, failing at something you or others think you can't do won't be fatal. Instead, it's the fear of failing when you think about doing something you have never done before that can be fatal.

More often than not, your dreams of doing the difficult, the daring, or the daunting will end up in failure, not because what was dreamed was impossible to do, but because your fear of failing kept you from ever tackling the task in the first place. As President Franklin D. Roosevelt said, "The only thing we have to fear is fear itself."

If you are going to ever allow fear to possess, guide, or motivate you, it should be the fear of mediocrity, fear of never excelling, fear of being the same person tomorrow that you are today. You'll never do the best you can't until your fear of being stuck in the status quo is greater than your fear of going broke, looking inept, being ridiculed, missing the mark, or any other form or fashion of failure.

You need to have the kind of philosophy expressed by Tom Cruise in his role as a victory-driven race car driver in the 1990 movie, *Days of Thunder*. He said, "I'm more afraid of being nothing than of being hurt." Those who have avoided "being nothing" almost always had some hurt or failure along the way. That failure or hurt was hardly ever as harrowing or horrific as first imagined. In fact, failure or hurt was often a boost rather than a barrier to success.

As mentioned in a previous chapter, in his book, *The Power of Positive Thinking*, Norman Vincent Peale espoused the idea that if you didn't quite make it to the moon when your goal was to reach that lofty height, you still had a good chance of landing among the stars. History is replete with stories of those who failed to reach their goal (the moon) but, not only did not find their failure to be fatal but, figuratively speaking, landed among the stars as a result of their failures.

A good example of the above is Dr. Spencer Silver, who was employed as a scientist at 3M. His failure turned out to be so fantastic that he was featured on *The Oprah Winfrey Show*. Dr. Silver said, "My job was to develop new adhesives, and the goal was to develop bigger, stronger, tougher adhesives." One of his experiments had just the right compounds formulated in just the right amounts with detailed documentation that would allow him to patent it and reproduce it gallon after gallon after gallon for purchase by 3M's industrial customers. Or so he thought. The fact was, when he let the formulation cool and stand over a period of time, it turned out to be so weak that he could stick two pieces of paper together and then peel them apart without tearing the paper. It did not even leave the sticky residue from one piece of paper on the other piece of paper.

Because Silver had invested hundreds of thousands of dollars in time, materials, and detailed documentation, he would not give up. For six years, he tried to either strengthen the weak glue he had developed or, alternatively, prove his inadequate invention had some practical use. He persisted but continuously failed to strengthen the weak glue. As a result, fellow researchers continuously rejected it. Its stickiness was too pitifully weak. They laughed at both his product and his stubbornness. They encouraged him to walk away from his product and cast aside all the useless data compiled throughout its formulation.

Indeed, it seemed like expense and effort was wasted and doomed to total failure when Art Fry, another 3M scientist, changed the outcome. Was it luck, coincidence, happenstance, or what some would call divine intervention? You see, Fry's church conducted choir practice each Wednesday night. They rehearsed the songs they planned to perform on Sunday mornings. Fry tore off little slips of paper to mark the pages they were to turn to each Sunday. Inevitably, the slips of paper would fall out of the hymnal, and Fry would struggle to find the next song. He remembered Silver had a weak glue that he might use to keep the slips of paper from falling out of Sunday's songbook, but without permanently sticking to or damaging pages on which the glue-coated slips were placed.

Fry and Silver refined the glue a little more and decided they could stick slips of paper with notes written on them on 3M documents and other interdepartmental and intercompany papers. It just so happened that when they began their internal use, there was a big box of yellow scrap paper they could coat and then cut into small pieces upon which to write their notes. Thus, in 1980, Post-it Notes were born from six years of failure. They were so useful and popular internally, the company decided to sell them to external entities. By 1996, this product was so popular that it had been accepted worldwide, with foreign sales surpassing 50 percent of all the revenue generated by Post-it Notes.

Today, Post-it Notes are sold in numerous colors, shapes, and sizes, all the way up to Post-it Easel Pads. A study of the American workplace determined that an average of eleven messages written on Post-it Notes are received each day by almost every company's professional staff. That adds up to more than $1 billion in annual sales. No wonder

Oprah Winfrey wanted to feature the failure of Dr. Spencer Silver on her television show!

How many companies would have fired Dr. Silver after his first year of failure, never refining and finishing what turned out to be a billion-dollar product? In the companies I've led over the years, I've felt failure should be applauded, not admonished. Innovation emanates from incentivizing risk-taking, not from discouraging it. I've always wanted my associates to feel free, fearless, autonomous, entrepreneurial, empowered, and encouraged to try stuff, even if it had "never been done that way before." Or if it had never been done at all. I wanted associates to feel that rocking the boat and taking risks would be rewarded, not rejected. I wanted them to feel that failure was not fatal to their future. Failure would be seen as simply a stepping-stone leading to improvement, innovation, and ultimate competitive advantage. Failure would result in being pushed up, not pushed out of the company.

Failure certainly ended up getting engineers Marc Chavannes and Al Fielding a promotion when they worked at Sealed Air Corporation. In 1960, they created what they thought would be a trendy textured wallpaper that would take the home and office decoration world by storm. Designers, decorators, and developers had their doubts. Sales suffered. Well, maybe their creation could be sold as insulation for greenhouses. Again, purchases were pitifully poor. After three straight years of low sales and high losses, maybe it was time to pull the plug on their product.

Yes, bubble wrap started as an abject failure. But, in the early to mid-1960s, IBM had begun to ship a lot of sensitive and fragile computers and components connected therewith. Poor packaging led to the discovery of damaged goods at destinations across the world. Maybe bubble wrap could provide protection during shipping. As is said, the rest is history. Today, over $400 million of bubble wrap is sold annually. That's enough bubble wrap sold each year to stretch from the earth to the moon. And not only does this product provide protection for breakables, but popping those air pockets is a stress reliever for adults and fun and games for kids.

Another product failure that wasn't fatal involved a literal goal of helping spaceships reach the moon. In fact, this failure—put an *s* on failure—turned out so positive that the product was named for the number of times it took to finally get it right. It was 1953. Rocket Chemical Company was working on a substance that would protect the outer skin of the Atlas Missile from rust and corrosion caused by moisture. Through the thirty-ninth attempt at formulating what was referred to as a water displacement solvent, nothing was adequate. Eureka! Attempt number forty fostered no more frowns. While it was meant for use for industrial purposes, more and more employees of Rocket Chemical Company began individually to use what became a perfect product produced after thirty-nine failures. It became so popular that in 1958, the company decided to package it in aerosol cans and sell it to retail customers.

You have probably bought WD-40, but I'll bet you never knew the name came from the company's desire to honor the persistence it took to overcome failure after failure after failure at creating a *water displacement* substance. Of course, you would never have been able to buy your first container of WD-40 if the laboratory had given up after thirty-nine failures.

If you think thirty-nine failures are a lot, how about 5,002? Five thousand of the failures were internal, and two were external. The first external failure occurred when James Dyson bought a vacuum cleaner that didn't work as promised. While vacuuming his home, Dyson discovered that instead of sucking in the dust and retaining it inside the vacuum, a large amount of the dust would escape back into the room. On top of that, whenever the dust and dirt the vacuum did retain began to fill the machine, the sucking power was diminished. He thought he could improve upon such a product. Thus, in1979, Dyson developed his own vacuum cleaner that overcame the deficiencies he'd discovered in others. However, the final product did not come about until he had developed more than five thousand prototypes. On top of that many internal failures and the frustrations that followed, he faced one more failure. It was external.

Dyson's many attempts to get other makers of vacuum cleaners to manufacture his model met with rejection after rejection. As a result of his failure to convince these companies to become colleagues, he had no choice but to make them competitors. If there was ever a "zero to hero" event, Dyson's determination definitely describes it. He not only used the technology in his vacuum cleaners to build a superior rug and floor cleaner but also incorporated his technology into appliances such as air purifiers, hand dryers, bladeless fans and much more. And today, Dyson employs some twelve thousand people and has annual sales of $7.3 billion (yes, that's a *b*).

Here are a few other stories I can share with you about failures that not only did not become fatal; they actually became fortunes:

- Wheaties exist because in 1921, a health clinician spilled a huge vat of gruel he was cooking for the patients on his ward. When the mixture met hot metal and fire, it turned into crispy flakes that were a lot more tasty than the mush he was making.
- Penicillin has saved millions of lives since bacteriologist Alexander Fleming returned from his vacation in 1928 to find that some dirty petri plates he failed to clean before leaving had grown mold. He was unhappy about having to start his return to work by washing dirty dishes. That is, until he saw that the mold had killed the staphylococcus bacteria he had also failed to dispose of before vacationing. Penicillin has killed lots of staph and other bacterial infections since that day.

- Synthetic dyes and the color mauve came about in the mid-1850s because a young scientist failed at making quinine from coal tar. Experiment after experiment failed to give him what he set out to produce. But from the mess he made emerged a pool of purple with a strange shade he had ever seen before. He realized he could dye fabric from his concocted color and built a small factory to do just that. When Queen Victoria saw this new color, she insisted on having a gown dyed therewith. Soon, "commoners" in Great Britain wanted to copy the queen, and thereafter the whole world was motivated by mauve.
- Home Depot exists today because Bernie Marcus and Arthur Blank faced what many would consider the most feared failure of all—getting fired. As Arthur Blank says in his book, *Good Company*, "Getting fired by Handy Dan (April 14, 1978) was a shock but turned out to be the best thing that could have happened to us." Without jobs or income, they were forced to figure out their future. Indeed, that future turned into fortunes. Both became billionaires.
- Do your own research into pacemakers, Nintendo, Apple and many other famous products and entities, and you'll be encouraged to do the best you can't, because you'll see that numerous well-known enterprises came into being because of failures that were not fatal.

Like the previous examples, a failure I endured with that little sixty-six-member church's mission to raise $400,000 for an exhibit at the New York World's Fair turned out to be fortuitous rather than fatal. Perhaps you will recall that I said our exhibit drew more visitors than any other religious exhibitor in the pavilion we occupied. That included the Billy Graham Association, Baptist, Methodist, Lutheran, Presbyterian, Episcopal and other religious groups that were better known "household names." And, unlike the Church of Christ, they had national and international boards to bolster them financially and otherwise. Having no national headquarters to which I could turn is the reason I had to drive all over the United States visiting individual, autonomous Churches of Christ in hopes I could convince them to make a contribution toward our effort to exhibit at the World's Fair.

What a nasty night. The darkness was made drearier by drizzle. Thankfully, it wasn't a downpour, as my windshield wipers weren't working well. I was driving rural roads to get to a fundraising meeting in Nashville because I had no choice. You see, back roads, local roads, rural roads were almost all that existed. The interstate system was in its early stages. Less than 10 percent of these concrete corridors that ultimately crisscrossed our nation had been completed. Not only was the freeway a future feature hard to find at that time, other things we take for granted today were not to be found at all. No personal computers. No emails. No cell phones. No text messages. No GPS to give driving directions. To find my way, I was dependent upon a multifolded, printed piece of paper.

Road maps are hard enough to read in bright daylight. I had to figure out where I was and where I was going by looking at my map when I drove through a town that was big enough to have a streetlight or two. That's because the overhead light in my car was not working, and I didn't carry a flashlight in my glove compartment.

I had scheduled a meeting with elders who had oversight of a Church of Christ with a thousand members. That's huge among Churches of Christ. Congregations average around 150 members. The elders were set to hear my story. They were capable of contributing $10,000–$20,000 if they liked what they heard. That would be my single biggest donation since I set out on my trek to raise $400,000. From Nashville, I was driving to Dallas, Texas, where there were some other fairly large congregations I might be able to motivate to match the monies from my meeting in Nashville.

It's eight o'clock. My appointment is at 7:30. Not only am I late; I'm lost. No cell. Thus, I can't call and apologize to the elders. I can't ask them to patiently wait on me. This causes a hundred negative thoughts to enter my mind: "They must be thinking I'm not dependable. Not reliable. Untrustworthy. Inept. They're saying, 'Bud should have told us days ago that he had to cancel the meeting. What a waste of our time. If this is the kind of leader this church has, then it would be irresponsible to give to their project.'"

Wait. There's a little encouragement ahead. A major intersection. Bright lights. Gas stations on two corners. One has a flashing neon sign. For late and lost pitiful little me, its message could not be more meaningful. It's offering "free directions at the push of a button." Inside, I discover a machine about the size of a standard jukebox. It contains an alphabetical listing of five hundred towns and cities across America. Rotate the list until you find the city to which you need to travel. There is an arrow inside the machine's glass encasement. The instructions say to point the arrow to your desired destination. Then, push the green "go" button. I do.

I hear a whirring sound and see gears turning inside the machine. *Slam! Bam! Wham! Presto!* Like magic, a slot in the machine spits out a piece of paper the size of a 3x5 index card. The paper says to take State Highway 9 south to County Road 22, then west to Federal Highway 301 and you'll reach the Nashville city limits. "Hey, this is neat. Even fun. I'll place the point of the arrow on Dallas, Texas, my next destination." Again, I hear the whirring sound and see the grinding gears. Another piece of paper spits out, this time with a list of roads and highways to Dallas. No road map required! Perhaps I was experiencing a tiny taste of the computerized world yet to come.

Standing in that nondescript gas station, a thought hits me. What if the church could buy one of these machines for our exhibit at the World's Fair? What if the arrow inside could point to something other than towns and cities? What if it could point to five hundred questions about the Bible? I conjure up questions like, who is the oldest man in the Bible? I imagine I can hear the whirring sound and see the grinding gears. My mind sees the machine produce a piece of paper printed with the answer: "And all the days of Methuselah were nine hundred sixty and nine years and he died." (Genesis 5:27, KJV) Wow! Here's another question: If you have enough power to understand all mysteries and enough faith to move mountains, what other characteristic does the Bible say you need or you really amount to nothing? The printed piece emerges from the machine and simply says, "Love." (I Corinthians 13:2, KJV) I can't resist conjuring up one more question and visualizing another answer. But one more does not satisfy me, so I stand there preparing question after question and programming answer after answer.

Talk about being like a turtle and sticking one's neck out; that's what I do next. It might have led to my arrest or at least to getting kicked out of the gas station. Without asking permission, I pull the machine away from the wall and climb behind it, looking for a tag disclosing the manufacturer or distributor. Where's a name? An address? A phone number? Where's the contact information that I can use to ask whether the machine can be loaded with my Bible-based inquiries instead of with road routes?

Hallelujah! I see a tag with the information I need and write it down before management catches me messing with their machine and calls the cops. The company is in New Jersey, right across from where I'm located in New York City. I plan a personal visit with them as soon as I get back from my fundraising trip to cities their machine told me how to get to.

Yes, I failed to see the elders of that big Nashville church, but you better believe I made the meeting with the machine's manufacturer. That resulted in two very positive outcomes. One, they could and would program my Bible-based questions and answers. Two, I convinced them that the number of people visiting our exhibit from around the world would give their machine the kind of exposure and publicity they could never afford to buy. Therefore, don't sell us your machine. Donate it. And when it needs paper added to it or needs maintenance or repairs, do it for free. Hey, you're right across the river from us, so that should be quick and easy. We didn't spend a dime for or on that machine that differentiated us from dozens of denominations.

Speaking of publicity, because I would not give up after several failures, I secured, free of charge, a discussion of our machine on *The Johnny Carson Show*. Most of those reading this book have probably not heard of Georgie Jessel. He was a pretty big celebrity in the 1950s, '60s and '70s. George Albert "Georgie" Jessel was an actor in Broadway plays and Hollywood movies. He was also a writer, composer, and producer whose skills as a dinner speaker earned him the honorary title of Toastmaster General of the United States. While not as famous as Bob Hope or Red Skelton, he was best known as a comedian and was sometimes compared to those two superstars. Georgie was slated to appear on *The Johnny Carson Show* right at the start of the World's Fair. After Georgie's comedy routine, he would sit down for a chat with Johnny. Now, wouldn't it help our little church draw crowds to our exhibit if Georgie would tell Johnny about this machine that has answers to five hundred Bible-related questions? Wow, what a great idea. Millions of people would be informed.

Well, this little naïve kid figured that all I had to do was call Georgie, tell him about our unique exhibit, and ask him to bring it up in his dialogue with Johnny. I called his office; his agent was there and took my call. He not so gently told me Georgie was "too busy to talk to any old Tom, Dick, or Harry he had never heard of." I called a second time in hopes I would get to talk to someone else who would not be so dismissive. I was rejected again. Then again. Then again and again and again and again. Finally, on the eighth call, a nice lady said she would get in trouble if she transferred me to Georgie. However, she wanted to be helpful and had a plan that might work. If I would call right back after she hung up the phone line she and I were on, she would make sure to be on another line so she could not answer my call. Since she and Georgie were the only two people in the office at that time, there was a chance Georgie would see she was on another line, and to avoid the incessant ringing from my call, he might personally answer the phone. No guarantees, she said, but he had been known to occasionally do that.

Bingo. It worked. After Georgie picked up the phone and I explained what I hoped he would do, he gave me two pretty valid objections. First, he was paid big money to make endorsements, and I was offering not a nickel. Second, he reminded me that he was Jewish and was not interested in pushing the Christian religion. I answered his objections as best I could. I asked him if he ever gave money to charities or other good causes. When he replied in the affirmative, I told him how fortunate he was to have an opportunity to give to another worthwhile cause, only this time he would not have to write a big fat check. His contribution would be his conversation with Johnny. Then I explained that the Jewish religion and the Christian religion stood for some similar values and that many of the questions in our machine would be answered by chapters and verses from the Old Testament. Jews follow the Old Testament, don't they? After a relatively short conversation, he invited me to visit him at his Manhattan office so he could gather more information about the Church of Christ exhibit and the marvelous machine we planned to feature. I went. I shared. He went to Johnny's show. He shared. Awesome advertising attained that we couldn't afford. All for free.

I'm still not sure why Georgie Jessel invited me to his office and agreed to assist me. Maybe my answers to his objections were powerfully persuasive. Maybe just my having the gall to call motivated him. Maybe curiosity about this Southern-sounding small-town kid who chose to live and work in New York City got the best of him. Whatever the reason, my success with man and machine happened only because of my earlier failure to make it to a meeting.

There have been other fundraising functions in which I was engaged. One epitomizes the "aim for the moon and fail at that, but as a result, land among the stars" philosophy. My friend Archie Crenshaw, whom I met while I was a student at Lipscomb University, telephoned me to request that I have lunch with him and Jimmy Faulkner, for whom Faulkner University, a Christian University in Montgomery, Alabama, was named. They wanted me to serve on Faulkner University's board of trustees.

This was a few years after my work with the church and the New York World's Fair. I now lived in Atlanta and had become an entrepreneur who over the years had founded a couple of somewhat successful companies. I had just sold one of my companies to a London Stock Exchange firm that wanted to do business in America and saw my enterprise as an excellent entryway. I told Archie and Jimmy they didn't really want me as a board member. Instead, they wanted a contribution. They were aware I had a nickel in the bank from the sale of my company. Archie assured me they were interested in my wisdom, my advice, my experience. Not my money. Now, Archie is a dear friend and an honorable soul with whom I'd entrust my life. But that was the biggest lie he ever told. It's okay, Archie. You didn't trick me. I knew all along you wanted my money, and I gladly gave it.

At my first Faulkner University board meeting, I learned we had endured six straight years of deficits. None of our staff or faculty had received a raise over those years. On too many occasions, their paychecks were several days late. On top of that, we were in arrears to our vendors by some 180 days. We were out of compliance with the terms of a bank loan. The balance sheet was weighted down with liabilities. I told the other board members it looked like I had joined the Titanic rather than a university board. I also said we ought to be ashamed to pay our bills late and that Christians are supposed to be reliable, dependable, and trustworthy. Then I made two commitments.

One, I'd make what was, for me, a substantial contribution if nine other board members would personally give or raise the same amount within 90 days. I told them that if those nine others would not match my gift, I'd give it to another cause. I had sold a company and felt an obligation, a happy one, to give a part of the proceeds to a worthy endeavor. However, if they would not help me get the school back on firm financial footing, then Faulkner didn't deserve to be that endeavor.

Second, I committed to dedicating the next ninety days of my life to seeking contributions from prospective donors the university would suggest I contact. One name on the list they gave me was John Amos, the founder, chairman, president, and CEO of Aflac Insurance (yeah, the company with the duck advertisements). In addition to being a business titan, he was also a (nonpracticing) lawyer. Because of his legal background, he had been invited to speak to one of our university's law school graduating classes a few years prior. That was not much of a connection to our university, but it was all I had to go on.

When I called Aflac to set up an appointment to see Mr. Amos, his administrative aide wanted to know the purpose of my visit. I knew if I told her I wanted to raise money for Faulkner University, she would not arrange a meeting. Because of Mr. Amos' wealth, everybody and his cousin were asking him for money. She couldn't say yes to another beggar. Thus, I told her very politely that I understood her job was to find out why people wanted to see Mr. Amos and limit visitors to a very select and important few. I commended her for doing her job in a friendly but firm fashion. However, I said I could only tell Mr. Amos the subject matter I wanted to discuss. I couldn't disclose it to her. Under those circumstances, she said she just could not set up an appointment. I told her I understood and would appreciate her delivering one message to Mr. Amos: that he was missing out on the opportunity to smile many times over many years if he did not give me an appointment. Within ten minutes of hanging up, she called me back. "Alright," she said. "Mr. Amos is curious about the many smiles over many years. He will give you fifteen minutes, and you better not waste his time." With the terrorist threats and kidnapping dangers that exist now, I wonder, if Mr. Amos were still alive today, would I, as a total stranger, get in front of him today as I did back in 1988?

What an office. It looked like it was as big as the half-acre lot on which my house sat. His desk was huge and was high on a stage that looked similar to a throne on which a king would be elevated or a platform on which a pulpit would sit in a church. If that was not intimidating enough, his very first words were. "This had better be good," he gruffly said. Full of fear, but also daringly determined, I proceeded to tell him about Faulkner University's need for capital. If he would help us educate the minds and strengthen the values and morals of kids, he would have hundreds of reasons to smile over the many years these students would add value to the workplace and to society in general. Remember, I got to see Mr. Amos because I said he would miss a lot of opportunities to smile if he did not meet with me.

Before I could finish my presentation, Mr. Amos said, "I'm sold. I'll be happy to contribute $500." I responded by saying, "Mr. Amos, you are neither sold nor happy, or you'd give a whole lot more than $500. It's obvious I did a poor job of explaining our needs and your opportunities. Now, I understand you can throw me out of your office, although that won't be necessary, as I'll leave if you ask me to. But I'm not leaving with $500. It might be zero, but I repeat, I'm not leaving with $500. It just won't help enough."

Mr. Amos said, "You are turning down my donation?"

"Yes, sir," I said. He replied, "I've never had that happen at any time in my entire life. So, let me tell you what I'll do. I'll give you $5,000."

I repeated what I had said a minute before. "Mr. Amos, I understand you can throw me out of your office, although that won't be necessary, as I'll leave if you ask me to. But I'm not leaving with $5,000. It might be zero, but I'm not leaving with $5,000. It just won't help enough."

Mr. Amos turned red in the face and said, "What size contribution are you seeking?" I replied, "A million dollars."

Now somewhat agitated and irritated, Mr. Amos responded, "Either you are crazy or you think I am. It takes estate planning to give a million dollars. I've got no interest in sharing any of my estate with Faulkner University. I am Catholic. You are Protestant. I don't even remember speaking at your law school, as you said I did. However, because you feel so strongly about receiving significant help from me, I tell you what I'll do. I'll give you $50,000, and if you tell me you will leave here with nothing before you will accept my $50,000, you'll be absolutely right. Now, what do you say to that?"

I answered his question thusly. "Mr. Amos, I want to thank you for your $50,000 gift."

He, in turn, asked to what address he could mail his check. I told him it would really help the university's cash flow if we didn't have to wait for the postal service to deliver his contribution. I'd like to take his check with me and hand deliver it to the school. Hearing that, he picked up his phone, buzzed his assistant, and said, "Make out one of my personal checks for $25,000 to Faulkner University. Add one of our company's checks for $25,000, and bring them for me to sign. Then, get this SOB (he didn't use the initials) out of my office."

Please, don't judge John Amos harshly because I shared with you the profanity he used. He said it with a somewhat teasing tone. And, to this day, I view him as a generous giant, not only to Faulkner University, but to scores of other good causes.

While I failed to reach my million-dollar goal (the moon), I felt $50,000 had landed me somewhere among the stars. The university certainly had no complaints, as my efforts during the ninety days of volunteer fundraising, along with the challenge I gave nine board members to match my gift, netted some $1.5 million. And it cost the school nothing in salaries, travel expenses, or consulting fees.

Some thirty-four years later, with a great deal of pride in Faulkner University, I'm happy to say we have had only two years where we spent more than the revenue we generated. However, the shortfalls were covered by a multimillion-dollar reserve we built for just such occasions. No late paydays have occurred since then. Invoices are always paid on time. Additionally, our law school has been accredited by the American Bar Association so our graduates can practice law in all fifty states, not just in Alabama where we are domiciled. Since then, we have also built a new business school building and now offer an MBA and other master's degrees in business. In 2021, we expanded our campus by some nine acres and constructed a building to house our new College of Health Sciences, offering degrees that focus on serving those impacted by autism—a $7+ million-dollar investment to serve this growing need.

From all the foregoing examples, I hope you see that failure is often a friend, not a fatal foe. Teachers in fifth-grade classes at Cannon Elementary School in Grapevine, Texas, believe this so strongly that they have their kids study biographies of people who have failed. Their work received national peer-review recognition in the January, 2021, *Science and Children* journal. One teacher, Joe Parthemore, was quoted as saying, "They (the children) were seeing how some of these people failed over and over and that its part of the learning process."

This lesson was emphasized in an article in the sports section of the March 20, 2021, *Atlanta Journal-Constitution*. It informed the readers that the University of Georgia's football team had such outstanding cornerbacks the previous season that it lost almost all of them to the National Football League's draft. It left such a shortage of defensive backs that Coach Kirby Smart had to take one of his offensive players, a star running back, and convert him to a defensive position, cornerback. In describing the process of training an offensive player to become a defensive player, Coach Smart disclosed that while the trainee (my terminology) had made a lot of good plays in practice, a lot of bad plays had also occurred. Smart surmised that it wasn't totally fair to take a fellow who had never defended against pass plays and have him face some of the best receivers on the Georgia team during spring practice sessions. "But," Coach Smart was quoted as saying, "that's how you grow and that's how you get better, by failing."

It's ironic that the highest honor a major league baseball pitcher can receive each year, the Cy Young Award, is named after a pitcher of yesteryears who holds the record for the most career losses (316) in major league baseball. Of course, the award is named after him because he also holds the record for the most wins (511) in major league baseball. in order to have a lot of successes, he had to endure a lot of failures along the way.

Speaking of baseball players, Hank Aaron didn't hit a home run every time he came to bat. He struck out more times than the number of home runs he hit. Strikeouts equaled 1,383. Homeruns equaled 755. He is beloved as a homerun hero today because he didn't let fear of failure—striking out—keep him out of the batter's box. Psychologist Dr. Henry Link said, "We generate fears while we sit. We overcome them by action." Thankfully, Hank Aaron got off his rear end and took action!

As Oprah Winfrey said, "Do the thing you cannot do. Fail at it. Try again. Do better the second time. The only people who never tumble are those who never mount the high wire. This is your moment. Own it."

Why not own it? Surely you won't fail as often as, say, Milton Hershey of chocolate fame. He started four candy companies that failed, and he filed for bankruptcy protection before finally getting it right on his fifth business attempt. Another famous fellow, J. C. Penney, filed for bankruptcy after his first store failed. Henry Ford's first two automobile companies failed spectacularly. Maybe nobody had as many failures as Abe Lincoln. His business failed in 1831. He was defeated for state legislator in '32. He had a nervous breakdown in '36. He was defeated for Congress in '43. Defeated again in '48. He lost a U S Senate race in '55. Lost his run for vice president in '56. Lost another senate race in '59. Was elected president of the United States in 1860.

The lesson you and I should learn from this chapter is that failing to achieve, even multiple times, is not the same as achieving failure. You see, we are not finished when we are defeated; we are finished only when we quit. So go ahead. Stick your neck out. Walk the plank. Do the best you can't. You probably won't fail, but if you do, it won't be fatal.

CHAPTER 6

YOU'VE GOTTA PREDICT THE FUTURE

You Don't Have to Be a Fortune-Teller,
Soothsayer, or Prophet to Do It

You CAN DECIDE THAT THE theme of this book is 100 percent right—that it is both desirable and possible to do the best you can't. You can be inspired by examples of people who did what couldn't be done. People like Rosa Parks, Steve Welker, Rusty Redfern, Bill Porter, and others who were discussed in Chapter 2. You can decide to stick your neck out. You can decide to walk the plank. And you can overcome any fear that's holding you back by realizing that failure is seldom fatal. However, unless you become a prophet and foretell the future in great detail, your dreams and desires will likely go unfulfilled. Your goals will be no more than wishful thinking.

But, you say, I am a mere mortal. I'm missing a messianic mind. I'm not an inspired individual imbued with a special strength to see the unseen and know the unknown. I thought this was a book of reason and reality, not one that delves into religious realms beyond my human reach. Whoa! Stop the stressing. You don't have to possess providential power to predict the future.

You foretell the future by the simple act of inventing it. You create it. You plan it. For example, you can predict you will get up and walk outside at two a.m. tomorrow. All you have to do is predetermine that is your goal, set your alarm clock, get up, put on your robe, and walk into the night air. Your prediction will come true because you had a plan that you executed. Yes, you can predict your exact whereabouts hours before you are there.

A freshly baked cake doesn't happen by happenstance. It doesn't happen haphazardly. There has to be a *plan*, even though that's not the word that's used. It's called a recipe. You can predict that a cake will appear about an hour after a certain plan (recipe) is followed. Just mix the right amount of flour, milk, eggs, butter, sugar, and flavoring. Pour it into a pan large enough to hold the ingredients after they expand (rise). Put the ingredient-filled pan in an oven at a temperature that is predetermined to cook the liquid-like mixture for a specific amount of time. The end product turns out to be a soft but somewhat solid creation called a cake. No abracadabra involved. You predicted a cake, and you got it. You foretold the future. You achieved what you set out to achieve because you had a workable plan and followed it.

If you have pneumonia, your doctor can predict you will get over it in fourteen days. But it takes a plan. It's called a prescription. Take three pills each day for fourteen days in a row. One at breakfast. One at lunch. One at dinner. You must follow the plan precisely for the prediction to come true. There are no shortcuts. You cannot take four-teen pills per day for three days instead. You can't let the container of pills sit unopened in your medicine cabinet for fourteen days. Your doctor can foretell your future wellness, but only if she devises a plan and you follow it.

Many of us would enjoy seeing America's countryside by leisurely driving from, say, Atlanta to San Francisco. Oh, what beautiful sights to savor. The goal, San Francisco, won't be reached by jumping in your car and taking the first road you see. Do that, and you might end up in Boston. To reach San Francisco instead of Boston, you must have a plan (using a map or GPS). Otherwise, you are like the bumper sticker I once saw that said, "Don't follow me; I'm lost." How many hapless humans are like that? In motion. Speeding along. Burning fuel. Expending energy. But not able to reach a desired destination because none was predetermined detail by detail.

It takes a literal or figurative road map, whether you are going to San Francisco, or going to lose weight, or going to earn all A and B grades, or going to quit smoking, or going to win a promotion, or going to learn to sew, or going to start a company, or going to strengthen a shaky relationship, or going to read a certain number of books a year, or going to qualify for a driver's license, or going to save money, or going to learn how to play a banjo, or going to make your spouse feel especially special, or ... or ... or ...

Almost anything you want to achieve takes a detailed plan. That's true even in a simple social situation like having someone as a guest in your home. You don't get someone to show up at your house when you say, "Come see me sometime." They don't show up even though they answer, "Sure will." You see, there's no "sometime" on anyone's watch or calendar. Such generic verbiage lacks the specificity needed to make the event happen. It takes a plain but pinpointed plan like, "How about coming to my home for a backyard cookout on Thursday, October 21, at 7:30 p.m.?" You'd better find out if they like their steak rare, well done, or somewhere in between, because you've landed a guest if the answer is, "What's your address, and may I bring my wife?"

Unless you approach other activities—actually, all aspirations—by mapping out step-by-step details in the same way one should approach acquiring houseguests, don't expect to see success. Don't expect to see a sign with your name on it hanging outside a business just because you say, "One of these days, I'm going to start my own company." Don't think your clothes will soon start smelling fresh because you say, "I need to give up my smelly smoking habit." Don't expect a scholarship offer just because you say, "I hope to improve my grades before I graduate." Don't believe you are going to bond with your kids just because you say, "I'm going to engage in more activities with my family." You have to have a step-by-step plan to start a company, to quit smoking, to get all As on your report card, to create closer chemistry with your children, or to accomplish any other change or improvement to your life or lifestyle.

Indeed, on any of the above goals or a myriad of others you may want to achieve, if you fail to plan, you plan to fail. That's true even in selling. The Princeton Center for Applied Research found there is a 93 percent better chance of sells success if the salesperson *has a plan and follows it*. As J. C. Penney said, "Give me a stock clerk with a goal and I'll show you a man who will make history. Give me a man with no goals and I'll show you a stock clerk." Since a goal, if it's a well-thought-out plan, has such a high percentage possibility of producing a positive outcome, why would you not challenge yourself and map out a plan to do the best you can't? As Michelangelo said, "The greatest danger for most of us is not that we aim too high and we miss it, but that we aim too low and we reach it."

If you are going to aim high and hit your mark—do the best you can't—it will require more than casual contemplation. It will require more than an idea that furiously flashes through your thoughts. It will require more than wishful thinking. More than hopefulness. More than sentiment. More than shallow suggestions. Sailing west to get east was not a fast and fleeting fancy Chris conjured up on the spur of the moment. And if you want to be or do something you are not being or doing today, neither will it be a quick and easy fix. It will take profound planning.

Your plan must meet a strict standard. It must be intensely intentional. It must emanate from deep, sober, serious, reflective thinking that is purposeful and pervasive. Such a strict standard is best spelled out by using the word SMART as an acronym. Your plan needs to be SMART if it is going to be effective. I'll expound on this acronym below.

First, though, I confess I've never had an original idea in my whole life. This acronym is something I've used, and taught my business associates to use, my entire adult life. I don't remember where I first read about it or heard about it. You've probably seen it a gazillion times and don't remember when you first encountered it either. I repeat it because its never-aging practicality and usefulness has earned it every bit of the emphasis it has been extended. And sometimes, if we are going to be motivated to take action, we just need to be reminded of what we already know. So, I'm using someone else's acronym. But I'm using my verbiage, mostly born out of what I've practiced over many years, to describe the lessons I want you to learn and apply from each of the words in the acronym. I hope my version is helpful to you.

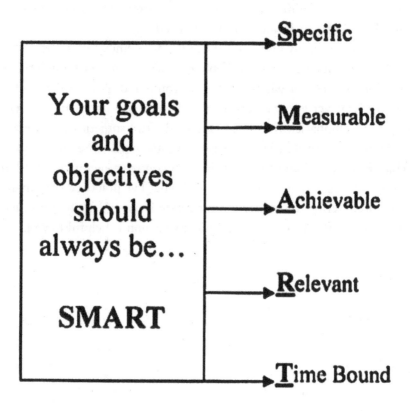

SMART plans are SPECIFIC.

Which salesperson is more likely to see an increase in prospective buyers? One that says, "I'm going to make a lot more sales visits this year than I made last year." Or one that says, "In order to see five more prospects each week during the coming year, I'm going to start each day one hour earlier than in the past. I'll use that hour I've added to each workday to make a presentation to an additional prospect."

Who is more likely to shed pounds? A person who says, "I'm going to lose some weight." Or someone who says, "In an effort to lose twenty pounds over the next six months, I'm not going to eat bread and butter with any of my meals; I'm going to have no desserts or fried foods on any day except the fourth Sunday of each month; and I'll have zero snacks between meals."

Who is more likely to build a cash reserve? A person who says, "I'm going to save some money this year." Or a person who says, "Instead of spending my annual salary increase, starting with my first paycheck in January and for the rest of the year, I'm going to put the full amount of my raise into a savings account that I'm going to open by the end of this week."

As previously written, you won't have a houseguest by inviting someone to "come see me sometime." Words like *sometime* are generic, not specific. Without specificity, there is little chance that change will take place, improvements will be made, tasks tackled, or ideas initiated. As the comedian and actress Lily Tomlin said, "I always wanted to be somebody, but now I realize I should have been more specific."

SMART plans are MEASURABLE.

If your goal is to "do more good" for others in the future than you have in the past, how do you know if you have accomplished that goal?

You can't know for sure because you cannot measure "do more good." Now, if you say that starting next Saturday, you are going to spend three hours every other Saturday tutoring three disadvantaged kids on their school assignments, you can measure whether you have met that goal. Because you can measure three and you can look at a calendar and find Saturdays, you can know (measure) whether you have "done more good." You can measure whether you have completely missed your goal, partially completed it, fully completed it, or exceeded it.

How do you complete the purchase of a service or a product? You complete a purchase when you have met the measure, that is, the price. If an item costs a dollar and you have a pocket full of pennies, your goal of securing the item won't be met until you pull one hundred pennies out of your pocket and give them to the seller. Not fifty pennies. Not ninety-nine pennies. Only when you fork over one hundred pennies to the seller will you know you have met your goal of purchasing the desired item.

The above principle involved in buying an item is a principle you must incorporate in your planning process. If you don't have an objectively discernable way to identify, count, or gauge progress toward your goals, you can't know if you have met them—if you have paid the price. If your goals are not measurable, you can't know what to shoot for or whether no more shots are needed because you have achieved your aim. Just as you must count and measure pennies to know if you have made a purchase, your plan must be countable and measurable to know if you are making progress toward or have attained your goal.

SMART plans are ACHIEVABLE.

This book is written to encourage its readers to do the best they can't. It's written to help you imagine the impossible and attain the unattainable. Thus, you are justified if you want to ask why SMART plans must be achievable, when the theme of this book is to convince people they can achieve the unachievable.

Without a doubt, I believe plans should involve dreams that are daring. Plans should involve reaching new records, hitting higher highs, surpassing long-standing standards. But plans should not be so far from reality's reach that they are guaranteed to end in futility, frustration, and failure. That's why people with common sense wouldn't dare to devise plans that call for walking ten miles in ten minutes, flying off the Empire State Building with just their arms as wings, or boiling an egg to hardness in 212-degree water in just two seconds. Plans that defy the laws of gravity or nature aren't SMART, because they aren't attainable. Short of that kind of ridiculousness, plans can be boldly bodacious and still be attainable.

SMART plans are RELEVANT.

Not long ago, a friend asked me to accompany him to view some acreage he was interested in buying. He decided to measure a field covered in tall grass and weeds by counting the number of steps it would take for him to traverse it from one end to the other. I told him I'd wait at the road's edge while he walked the field. As he was about halfway through his trek, I saw his cell phone falling from the encasement in which he carried it around his waist. I yelled to him that he had dropped his phone, but he was far enough away that he didn't hear me.

Fearing my friend might never find his phone on his way back to the road where I was waiting, I glued my eyes on the spot where I'd seen the phone fall and went to retrieve it. There was a lot of beautiful nature I could have viewed as I was headed to the spot where I saw my friend's phone fall. On the horizon was a majestic mountain topped off with tall timber. There was a brook bending beyond the bushes. We were far enough into the country that there had to be a beautiful bird or two to hold in awe. Maybe even a furry fox. However, I couldn't search for those sights. That's because there was nothing to distinguish the spot where the phone had dropped. No mound of dirt. No different-colored grass or taller weeds at that spot. If my stare did not stay exactly where I saw the phone fall, I would never find it.

As I walked, I could not even look down to avoid a hole that might trip me. I could not watch out for a limb or log over which I might stumble. Nothing was relevant to my goal except fixating my eyes on the exact spot on the field where the phone had fallen. I had to focus on one thing. All else was minor to my mission. If my plan had been to photograph the countryside, I would never have ignored the mountain, the brook, the birds, or the fox. But in the pursuit of the phone, they were irrelevant. I could not make them a part of the picture—the plan.

A SMART plan will focus on reaching the end result, just as I focused on the spot where the phone fell. Nothing should sidetrack the process or procedure that leads to a plan's completion. A hawk has sharp-enough eyes to see two rabbits at once. However, he never chases both at the same time because he knows if he does, he will catch neither. If you created a plan to learn how to play a piano, it would not be wise to also spend time learning how to play the flute. That would be irrelevant to your goal. The point, therefore, is to never let anything interfere with your plan's main thing. Stay focused. Stay relevant.

SMART plans are TIME BOUND.

There is no way to know if you will be great or lousy at fulfilling your plan if you never get started. There is certainly no way to finish if you never get started. You can never get started if you never start. So, don't tell yourself you plan to "soon" start exercising or _____ (fill in the blank). Whether your plan is exercising, reading a book, incorporating a company, or _____, tell yourself you are going to start at your lunch hour today. Or at eight a.m. Thursday. Or at daybreak on June 1.

"Soon" won't get you started on implementing your plan. "Lunch hour" will. Setting a specific time ties or binds you to beginning your plan. When your calendar and your clock reach the time you set, it will be a reminder that you must commence your commitment at that minute. It jogs your memory. It pricks your consciousness. It puts you into gear. It's the kick in the rear end that reminds you that you have a plan and it's now, and if you put it off, it may be never.

A starting time (year, month, day, hour, minute) is critical to your plan's success. An ending time could be just as critical. For example, fasting may be good for your health. However, if you fast forever, you'll eventually starve to death.

If you are going to formulate a successful plan, timelines should also include segments and stages between specific starting and ending times. That truth is illustrated by the question that has become a cliché: "How do you eat an elephant?". A plan to eat an elephant can be successful if it is "one bite at a time." Any other plan would probably be too much too soon. This same principle applies to, say, a plan to read a dozen books this year. You'll fail if your plan calls for starting at noon today and continuing until you've read the last word of the last chapter in the last book on your list of twelve. It's not physically possible to stay awake that long.

I plan to jog 1,095 miles this year. I'll be successful because I've put time boundaries around my goal. I won't do it all at once. I will start at the end of each workday and run three miles. I'll do it for 365 days in a row. By the way, three miles is nothing compared to the 54,750 miles I once jogged. Of course, "once" was time bound by starting with three miles per day and faithfully continuing that same distance every day for fifty years. Assuming I live a little longer, I'll cross the

55,000-mile mark, but only because my plan was/is set in stages or segments that are time bound.

You don't want to be like the fellow who committed suicide because he was overwhelmed at the thought that if he lived to be seventy, he would have to tie his shoes 25,550 times. He would not have thought that tying shoes was such a terrible task if he had reminded himself that he might not be able to tie his shoes 25,550 times, but that he could tie them once. Once a day was all it would take. He just needed to do it for seventy years. Tying shoes, jogging multiple miles, reading a list of books, or any other goal needs to be broken down into achievable time frames that are specifically enumerated. Such segments or stages make plans manageable and keep the end goal from looking so daunting that you think it's not doable.

Planning, if it incorporates the SMART acronym as described above, will promote positive outcomes in any area of life, whether it's business or personal. In business, I've always asked those who reported to me to create quarterly plans so they had specific goals at which to aim and step-by-step action items to help them hit what they aimed for. To make sure those plans were SMART, I required three things of my reports. By the way, I had the same three requirements for myself as well. After all, a manager should practice what she or he preaches. Below, I'll show you an actual quarterly plan I set for myself when I was CEO of an entrepreneurially driven insurance enterprise that grew from zero to $200 million in premium volume in ten years. Maybe my plan can serve as a model for you. Here are the three requirements that helped ensure my plans and my managers' plans were SMART.

(1) Commit the plan to written details. A plan is more likely to be SMART if it is outlined on paper. Lee Iacocca, who gained fame as the developer of the Ford Mustang and later became even more renown when he became chairman of Chrysler and saved it when it was on the brink of bankruptcy, said, "The discipline of writing

something down is the first step toward making it happen." Whether you are going to achieve the unachievable or just do what is difficult, there's no getting around the need for a SMART plan. There is no quick and easy way. No shortcut. Therefore, take the time to think through exactly how you will accomplish your goal. Then put yourself through the not very glamorous grind of putting your plan on paper.

(2) Before finalizing their plans, I had my colleagues share them with others who reported to me. This was done in a meeting of peers, all of whom had written plans. We went from person to person to ask if they thought their colleagues' plans were SMART. As each point of each plan was presented, we had fun shouting out "smart!" or "not smart!"

That was an effective way to improve the step-by-step means and methods our managers planned on using to conquer their individual goals. It would be wise for you to consider a similar disclosure of your plans, whether they be personal or business. After outlining your plan to do the best you can't, share it with one or a few other people and ask them to tell you what is "smart" and what is "not smart."

(3) At the end of each quarter, I'd again gather these managers in a group meeting—this time to report on whether they had missed, made, or exceeded the goals they had shared with one another some three months earlier. Everyone compared their actual accomplishments against what their written plan called for. The group would vote to award a certificate to the person whose plan they thought had turned out to be the most significant and accurate accomplishment of what had been put on paper. The vote decided the person whose plan had best achieved or exceeded what had been predicted some ninety days prior. The certificate was titled, "Perfect Performing Prophet of the Quarter."

A crisp $100 bill was also given to the winner. The winner appreciated the money, as it likely meant taking her or his spouse to dinner without having to personally pay for it. However, by a long shot, money was not the main motivator. The "Perfect Performing Prophet" certificate was the prestigious prize. It meant the recipient had invented a better future, described it in writing, and executed it so effectively that what she or he predicted came true.

The written plan of the "Perfect Performing Prophet" may not have been executed 1,000 percent perfectly, but it had been executed better than any other. Very talented and competitive fellow managers were saying, in effect, that the winner was the best manager this past quarter. Nobody wanted to look bad when reporting their quarterly results in front of eight or nine peers. It should be no surprise that our company was growing at 25+ percent per year. Our associates were motivated to predict and prophesize by way of a plan that outlined what activities and outcomes they intended to achieve each future ninety-day period, and how they would perform that plan as perfectly as possible. They predicted the future by inventing it, then describing it in written form, then executing every detail in the timeframe they allotted themselves to do so.

After sharing your written plan with people, as my managers did in (2) above, then, as in (3) above, you should set future dates with those same people for the purpose of reporting on how well you achieved your goals. Just as my managers did not want to disappoint me, their fellow managers, or themselves, you will not want to share disappointing results. You will have much more motivation to effectively execute your plan if others are aware of it and know how positively you are performing it.

Now, before I show you an actual past plan of mine as I promised to do a few paragraphs ago, I'd first like to reprint the instructions I requested that all my company colleagues follow in our planning process.

Information and Instructions for Quarterly Plan Preparation and Presentation

The sheet titled "My Desired Outcomes for the Next 3 Months" has a completed example by me. Hopefully, it will help you understand the information I am seeking from each of you. Please read this information/ instruction sheet before attempting to model your plan after mine.

+Business Outcomes/End Results: This is not meant to be totally exhaustive. Just list 3 to 4 important end results you will bring to completion. For example, if your goal is to appoint as a writer of our insurance policies the largest insurance agency in a particular county, you won't do that over and over again. Once the agency is appointed, you've achieved your end result.

+Leadership/Management Activities: Unlike above, these are not end results but on-going action items. For example, if your goal is to mail a handwritten acknowledgement and thank you note to agents who write at least 10 policies with us in a one week period of time, that never ends. You'll do that over and over as long as anyone is writing 10 policies a week with our company. This list of management/leadership activities is not meant to be exhaustive either, but should be some of the important action items in which you will be engaged.

+Personal Life Outcomes: This is not an attempt to pry into sensitive or confidential issues. Such are none of your company's business. However, your company is interested in the whole person—a balanced person who is not only improving while on the job—but is becoming healthier and happier at home, in the community and within the recesses of your own mind and body. Hopefully, this exercise will help you become a complete success, not just a success in business.

As you know, we will disclose and discuss our plans in our upcoming quarterly meeting. Your fellow managers will, in a very straightforward fashion, tell you whether they think your plans are smart or not smart. You will find sharing your business and personal goals with your colleagues helpful in at least two ways. First, they can help you improve your plan and its likelihood of success by offering suggested changes for you to consider. Second, you will not want to disappoint your colleagues when, at the end of the quarter, we meet together again. The purpose of this meeting will be to report on how well goals were achieved. In light of all of this, remember to make all your goals, projections and statements SMART (the acronym we have all discussed).

As promised, here is one of my quarterly plans.

Name: <u>BUD</u>

My Desired Outcomes for the Next 3 Months

Business Outcomes:
- No later than the 2nd week of the quarter, interview the first of at least 3 prospective firms or individuals that conduct company training programs on a contract basis. By the end of the quarter, select and formerly engage one of them to provide training to personnel at all levels of responsibility within AssuranceAmerica.
- During the first 30 days of the quarter, visit a competitor to discover their best practices in their claims department. Reciprocate by having them visit AssuranceAmerica during the next 30 days to discover our best practices in our claims department.
- Within the first 30 days of the quarter, buy a book on sales and/or management for each of my direct reports and ask them to be ready to discuss it at our quarterly meeting some 60 days later.

Leadership/Management Activities:
- Starting the 1st Thursday of the quarter and continuing each Thursday thereafter, between the hours of ten until noon, telephone 15 owners of agencies our Territory Managers visited the previous week. Thank the owners for the time given to our TMs and ask how we can better serve their agencies.
- Starting the 2nd week of the quarter, travel with a Territory Manager in her/his territory on Tuesdays and Wednesdays of the 2nd and 4th weeks of each month.
- Within 3 days of the above visits, mail a handwritten note to each of the customer service representatives, agents and agency owners with whom I engaged thanking them for their time and expressing appreciation for working with AssuranceAmerica

Personal Life Outcomes:
- Starting the first week of the quarter, on Mondays, Wednesdays and Fridays of each week add 60 arm curl weightlifting exercises to my daily 3-mile jog.
- Starting this week, eat red meat no more than once a week and eat fish at least twice each week.
- Starting this month, play a sit-down game (like dominos, checkers, monopoly) right after supper with my son and one of his friends the 1st and 3rd Saturdays of each month.

Writing out a SMART plan each quarter put me on a path of perpetual productivity. Because I had a detailed plan and dates for executing it, I had control over my business and personal outcomes. I became a prophet that could predict the future. My predictions came true.

Obviously, I had many responsibilities and activities to take care of that were not a part of my written plan—things like interviewing prospective hires, taking phone calls from those who wanted to talk with me, meeting with colleagues who wanted to discuss problems or opportunities, and a myriad of other activities that could not be planned, but which could fit into whatever hours and days were not filled beforehand. My SMART plan's main purpose was not meant to cover every minute of every day. Its main purpose was to outline how and when to accomplish some of the more major matters I needed to undertake each quarter.

Planning of the kind I have described requires more than the mental assent you may have given to all the chapters before this one. Those chapters had some interesting feel-good stories and illustrations. They shared some historic and heroic information. Perhaps they elicited emotional highs from you. Maybe they even inspired you to feel that the impossible is possible. All that is well and good, but feelings and emotions are often too abstract, general, theoretical, or philosophical to amount to more than considerations.

This chapter, however, is asking that you do more than emit feelings or emotions. Hopefully, this chapter plainly points out that if you want to accomplish the kind of spectacular achievements described in earlier chapters, that will occur only if they are preceded by un-spectacular planning and preparation. This chapter argues that you must go to the trouble to plan processes, procedures, ways, means, and timelines if you really want tomorrow to be better than today. It is an attempt to say that if you don't want to settle for being your same old self tomorrow that you are today and you don't want to stay stuck in the status quo, it will take more than considering, hoping, wishing, dreaming, and thinking. The path to progress requires that you take immediate action to write out a SMART plan. Indeed, it requires that you engage in some serious and sober planning—not someday, but today!

CHAPTER 7

SECRET OF SUCCESS SUMMED UP IN THREE LITTLE WORDS

The Main Thing to Do to Be Rich and Thin

FAIRLY FREQUENTLY, SOMEONE WILL TELL me how lucky I am not to have a problem with weight. My usual response is to use an expression I heard my momma say a zillion times, even though I'm not sure I totally understand it. Momma would say, "Luck, my hind foot. I work like a dog to stay in shape."

Hey, Momma, since your passing, I miss you for many reasons. One, I'd like to ask you, what's a hind foot? Two, other than in Alaska where they pull sleds through the snow, Momma, do dogs work hard? The rescued dogs my wife and I have adopted don't pull sleds. Our Chihuahuas not only don't pull sleds; as tiny as they are, they don't even pull their own weight. Eat a lot. Sleep a lot. Love a lot. But, work a lot? No!

Anyhow, keeping my height and weight proportionate has no more to do with luck than my having a hind foot. It has more to do with the fact that I work like one of those sled-pulling dogs. Stretching, slogging, steaming, straining, and sweating without ceasing is why I don't have a weight problem. Giving up all desserts and soft drinks many years ago has also helped keep me trim. So please, don't tell me how lucky I am. I've paid the price in the past and perpetually since.

And please don't say what I also often hear: "I know you love to jog. You do it so faithfully. I just don't love it the way you do, so it's not easy for me to keep the habit like it is for you." Love it my hind foot. It's a drain on my time and energy. It's boring. It's a terrible task. I hate every minute of jogging. But I do it because I love the end result. I endure the pain because of the gain. It takes determined discipline to do something I hate. However, knowing that I don't look like I'm eight months pregnant with quintuplets motivates me to pay the price.

Maybe more interesting than the way I've explained why I don't have a potbelly is to share with you an article about how much effort and energy I've put into exercising. It emphasizes how steady and hard I've worked and makes no mention of luck. That's because luck doesn't play a part. It's expending energy and exerting effort. Every day, not erratically. The article appeared in *The Dahlonega Nugget* on June 24, 2020, exactly two months before I turned eighty years old. Dahlonega is the hometown my wife and I adopted to live and die in soon after I retired (mostly retired, that is) from AssuranceAmerica, the automobile insurance company I cofounded with Guy Millner. Guy is an outstanding human being I am fortunate to call a friend, business mentor, and business partner. I'll tell you more about Guy in a later chapter if you promise not to be jealous and envious that I'm so blessed to be associated with such a super-successful specimen of business, philanthropy, integrity, and decency.

Matt Aiken, the publisher of *The Dahlonega Nugget*, titled the front-page article he wrote, "PUSHIN' 80." It reads as follows.

"Technically Bud Stumbaugh is a senior citizen. But only technically. 'I say I have the energy of a 40-year old,' he told *The Nugget*. 'It's easy to do the math since that's half my current age.' And you may have noticed that youthful energy on display on the roadways of Dahlonega as the soon-to-be octogenarian can be seen running in his trusty Nike Airs every day. Yes, every day. No matter rain or shine or coldness or sweatiness, he makes sure to clock in 3 miles a day. It's a workout regimen he started more than 50 years ago. And he hasn't stopped since. Back then Stumbaugh's motivation was simple. He didn't want to be Wilber.

'I was 30 years old and I came down the stairs for breakfast,' said Stumbaugh. 'And my six-year-old daughter Stacey was at the breakfast table and she didn't mean to be critical, but she pointed to my stomach and said, 'Daddy, you look like Wilbur.' Wilbur was a church member who was known for his impressive size. Or as Stumbaugh put it: 'Wilber looked like he was about eight months pregnant, and with quintuplets on top of that.' Stumbaugh did not want to be the next Wilbur. And so, he started to run. 'That afternoon I decided I'm going to start jogging,' he said. 'I probably went a quarter of a mile and that's all I could do I was so out of shape.' Now, 50 years later, the 79-year-old Stumbaugh could easily outpace his 30-year-old self. There's a good chance he could outrun his daughter too. The now Stacey Andrick said she and her husband are avid cyclists, but they still can't manage to keep up with the elder Stumbaugh. 'He can't sit still,' she said. 'We're strong and athletic and he stills runs circles around us.'

Even doctor's orders couldn't slow Stumbaugh for too long. 'Once I had surgery and the doctor said you cannot run for a month. And I took his advice,' Stumbaugh said, 'for a week.'

Stumbaugh stopped eating most sugars 10 years ago and he keeps his muscles toned by lifting weights four days a week. When asked if people are often surprised by his age, he said yes ... in a way. 'They're surprised because I look like I'm 100.' he said. 'Then they find out I'm actually almost 80. Then they realize that energy wise I'm about 40. So, they just have to go through those three stages.'

Stumbaugh's energy doesn't stop on the running route though. He's a motivational speaker and still holds down a regular job in Atlanta. 'I am really lousy at retirement,' he said. 'The first time I retired I was 48 years old.' That retirement lasted one month. Stumbaugh went on to start another company and retire at 55, before starting another company and retiring at 68.

'And I retired, I thought for the last time at 75,' he said. 'But my old company keeps calling me back for special projects, so I'm still working.'

That company is AssuranceAmerica Insurance Co, which is located on the sixth floor of an office building off I-285. Stumbaugh never takes the elevator. He often gets his run in around the office before jumping into his car for the long commute back home.

If Stumbaugh's name sounds familiar that could be because he served as a state senator from 1976 to 1990.

(They named a bridge after him.) He also ran for Lt. Governor in 1990 and campaigned by hiking around the entire state. He passed through Dahlonega that year and still remembers having a friendly chat with then sole-commissioner JB Jones.

The Alabama native said he's wanted to live in Dahlonega for years. And he and his wife Tania finally made the move about 19 months ago. Once he arrived here, he made his presence known by handing out a business card emblazoned with the slogan: 'This Bud's *really* for you.' He also jumped into the local volunteer scene with vigor as he's currently on the board for The Holly Theatre. Fellow board member Nathan Gerrells can attest to Stumbaugh's energy. 'He's a force of nature,' he said. 'I have seen him show up to board meetings in a track suit because he had to squeeze his run in before the meeting.'

That drive transfers to recruiting fellow volunteers as he serves as the Development/Fundraising Committee chair. 'It's almost impossible to tell him no,' said Gerrells.

Though he may be listed in the 'at-risk' category, Stumbaugh has jogged his way through the coronavirus era. Never faltering from his 3-mile run. He's concerned, of course, but not frightened. 'I'm going to do everything I can to take care of myself,' he said. 'But I'm not going to cringe at the possibility that something bad might happen.'

Andrick said she socially distanced from her father during this time period, but it wasn't easy. And though she was worried for her dad, she also took comfort in the fact that he's not the usual old-timer. 'I do think that if anyone in the whole world could beat COVID-19 as an 80-year-old, he'd be the one,' she said. Andrick added that her dad is an inspiration to her, and also her coworkers, as she once invited him to her workplace as a motivational speaker. 'I brag on him all the time,' she said. 'I'm very proud of him and I love him dearly.' When asked if she can take credit for her dad's healthy lifestyle change Stacey responded with a quick laugh. 'Exactly,' she said.

True to his motivational form Stumbaugh said his success isn't due to any kind of magic secret. Anyone can do it, he said. It's just about getting out there and actually doing it.

'Here's my philosophy,' he said. 'Don't worry about being better than others, or outpacing others, what you need to do is be better than yourself.'

Stumbaugh will officially turn 80 in August. He plans to celebrate by buying himself two new pairs of Nikes. And as he nears that landmark age, he admits that eventually he's going to have to slow down and take it easy. Just not in this life. 'I have very reluctantly given up the notion that I'll continue to jog three miles every day,' he said with a grin. 'After my funeral.'"

Here's a similar take on controlling weight. Robert Herjavec is a multi-multimillionaire and successful business owner. He is also one of the stars of ABC's television hit program, *Shark Tank*. In a broadcast of one of the shows he said, "Everybody wants to be rich. Everybody wants to be thin. But very few people want to put in the effort." I think he is absolutely right. In the long run, effort will determine effectiveness of outcome.

Hard work will beat talent. Hard work will beat giftedness. Hard work will beat high IQ. Hard work will beat luck. It will beat knowing the right people. It will beat growing up in privileged circumstances. And as important as education is, hard work beats that too. (You'll see in a later chapter that I don't diminish the importance of education. Just the opposite: I urge lifelong learning if you really want to do the best you can't.)

How hard work can lead to success is well illustrated by a story in the April 24, 2021, edition of the *Atlanta-Journal Constitution*. It chronicled some of the life of Dan Pitts, who upon his retirement was the winningest high school football coach in the entire state of Georgia. His record was 346 wins, 109 losses and 4 ties. What made this so remarkable was that he won all those games as coach of a high school in the tiny town of Forsyth, Georgia, population 4,100. He did not have anywhere near the number of talented boys to choose a team from as did coaches that could choose elite athletes from towns with populations of twenty-five, fifty, or seventy-five thousand.

One of Coach Pitts' rules was that before practice could end and everyone go home at the end of the day, each squadron of players had to run ten plays perfectly. Talk about doing the best you can't; perfection ten times in a row is almost impossible. But that requirement enabled the team to overcome whatever disadvantages they had in not being able to select players from a larger pool of potential superstars. Lack of size or speed could be overcome through sharpened execution.

David Sewell, quarterback on one of Coach Pitts' late 1970s teams, said, "Coach Pitts didn't know how to quit." And, Bill Bazemore, a center on one of his teams, said, "He taught us that hard work equals success, plain and simple. He taught all of us that. And when we worked hard, we were successful. And that translated into being a father, being a husband, being a professional."

On June 1, 2021, the Associated Press distributed another story about how hard work in the athletic arena pays off. It was about Alexis Roberts, who received an athletic scholarship to play basketball at Jackson State University. It was a first. Not a first scholarship granted by the university, as it has given thousands over the years. It was the first athletic scholarship given to a totally deaf person who was also unable to speak clearly since she has never heard words like most of us have heard and, as a result, learned to parrot. Her high school coach at the Mississippi School for the Deaf was quoted as saying, "At that level (university varsity team) it's a chance to let the world know any deaf person can do it. You just need the hard work, but sometimes the deaf people need to work a little bit extra hard, but you can make it happen and here is proof."

Alexis Roberts may not have had the opportunities, the resources, and the physical capabilities others had, but hard work put her at their same achievement level.

Doesn't that remind you of Zach Hodskins, about whom I wrote in Chapter 2? He was the young man from a small Georgia town who garnered headlines in the sports section of the *New York Times*. His feat was receiving a basketball scholarship to the University of Florida, even though he had no hand or forearm on one side of his torso. He would stay and practice shooting for hours after his teammates were finished. His one hand from which he could dribble and shoot would sometimes bleed from all the extra hours of effort. But hard work showed he could do what can't be done and earned him a scholarship in the process.

Coach Pitts', Alexis Roberts', and Zach Hodskins' approach to winning mirrors what Babe Ruth had to say: "It's hard to beat a person who never gives up." And American author, Og Mandino, expressed similar thoughts when he said, "Failure will never overtake me if my determination to succeed is strong enough."

George Bernard Shaw, the great poet who lived from 1856 to 1950, had an approach to action that has been the cornerstone of whatever successes I've had in my life. He said, "When I was young, I observed that nine out of every ten things I did were failures, so I did ten times more work."

That aligns perfectly with what I heard from a guest speaker at a civic-club luncheon I once attended. The speaker headed a personnel assessment company that administered aptitude tests—you know, the tests that tell people what they're fit for.

When the speaker finished his message, he asked if there were any questions. Several were asked. The most intriguing question was not so much because of the question. It was because of the answer. The speaker was asked, "Have you ever had anyone that totally failed your tests, that is, wasn't fit for anything?" He replied without hesitation. "Oh, yes. We keep very careful statistics, and we've found that one out of every 1,783 people who take our tests fail. They are fit for nothing. However, we never worry about these occasional rare failures. That's because, invariably, they are the boss. They own the company."

He continued to explain that at an early age, the "fit for nothing" person knew he had no talent. No appreciable aptitude. No special skills. Wasn't wired with wisdom. No advantageous attributes. So he doubled and tripled his efforts. Put in more time. Worked harder than anybody else. Nothing more than his diligence and determination made it possible for him to rise to the top and end up a winner.

The "fit for nothing" fellow was the opposite of the son whose father said that his boy's goal was to be a garbage man when he grew up. An acquaintance told the father that becoming a garbage man was an unusual ambition for a young boy to have. The father said, "Not really. He thinks garbage men work only on Tuesdays."

Certainly, the times in my life I've done the best I can't occurred mostly because, like the fellow described by the assessment tester, I was aware of my shortcomings and knew I had to work more than just Tuesdays.

Yes, realizing I have limited abilities, I know I have to outwork everybody else. It seems that in situations where I've done that, they should be a part of this book. However, in sharing some of my personal experiences with hard work, I risk coming off like a boastful braggadocio whose enormous ego is out of control. Actually, I believe just the opposite to be the case. Sharing stories about my hard work is acknowledgement that my brain, talents, skills, and competence are inferior to most other people's. It's an acceptance of the fact that I have to work harder than others because I don't otherwise match up to their strengths. Writing about my hard work is actually a show of modesty, because it's an admission that I have few other positive characteristics to emphasize.

Without a doubt, it was through hard work that I got my first job in the private-enterprise, for-profit world. From earlier chapters, you will remember that I had been in the nonprofit world. I was doing church work. Pay was pretty paltry. I wanted to earn more. I began to answer ads in the classified section of the newspaper.

Notwithstanding my lack of experience selling advertising and managing others who did the same, the national sales manager for a specialty advertising enterprise wanted to hire me. The job was district manager over the states of Tennessee and Kentucky. My responsibilities would involve managing the existing sales team plus recruiting, appointing, and training additional salespeople to fill empty territories. Recruiting and training would recur frequently because salespeople were paid by straight commission. That contributed to extraordinarily high turnover.

Before the national sales manager could hire me, he had to first get approval from the president/owner of the company. I traveled to the company's headquarters in anticipation of a friendly interview with the president. However, friendliness was not to be found. No warm welcome awaited me when I walked into his office. He had an intimidating glare. His voice was gruff. His attitude was antagonistic. He didn't start the conversation with the usual "Happy to meet you" salutation. Nor did he thank me for taking the time to visit him and his company.

The owner's first words were, "I cannot for the life of me figure out why we are wasting each other's time with an interview. You don't have the experience we need in a district manager. One of the salespeople in the district we are discussing has been with us for nineteen years and has been in his current territory all that time. He is fifty-seven years old, and you are twenty-six. He won't look up to you or listen to you because he has a hundred times more experience than you. Another salesperson in the district, the fellow we have in Nashville, has been our number-one salesperson in America for fifteen months in a row. You've never sold a nickel's worth of advertising, so your credibility with him will be zero. He's not naïve enough to think a church fellow can teach him anything."

My response was to tell the owner that I knew a way to gain almost immediate credibility. I was aware of a weekly newsletter the company mailed (this was before email existed) to all its salespeople each week. It always listed each salesperson's production, from the highest to the lowest. There were about a hundred salespeople across the united states, and the number-one producer's total sales for the week was published. That was also true for number two, three, four, and every number down to one hundred. Individual sales and the name of the person who produced them were listed from the most to the least. I told the owner I was aware of a territory that had no salesperson. "Put me there for one month and I'll sell enough that my name will show up pretty high on the weekly listing of producers. My name will be seen in a positive position for four weeks in a row. While one month is not a real long time, it should be enough to earn me at least a little credibility. I won't start as district manager with no record or reputation at all."

Was the owner snickering or scoffing at my suggestion? He certainly showed no sympathy toward the scenario I outlined. He reminded me that I had no training on their products, processes, or procedures. I hadn't listened to a sales presentation that had been either accepted or rejected. I wouldn't know how to answer objections. He argued that I wouldn't place in the top fifty in any of the four weeks.

Reminding him that he had nothing to lose by putting me in an empty territory, he finally acquiesced and gave me the sales script to learn and some contracts for buyers of our advertising to complete. His last words were, "You're not likely to fill in any of these contracts, so give them back to us when your little trial is over. They're expensive to print and I don't want to waste money."

I gave notice to the church and was proudly pounding the pavement three weeks later. And guess whose name was at the top of the newsletter list each and every week for the next four weeks? Yep, I was the fellow the other ninety-nine were reading about and looking up to. And when it was announced that I was the new district manager over Tennessee and Kentucky, instead of rejecting me, my more experienced sales team was asking me how in the world I achieved the number-one ranking for four weeks in a row.

Well, I cheated. Oh, not in a dishonest or unethical way. I just did not stay within the company's guidelines. You see, salespeople were told to call on prospects Monday through Friday only. Our standard *modus operandi* was to walk door to door calling on business owners without an appointment. It's called cold calling. We were taught it was a waste of time to sell on Saturdays because few owners worked that day. That meant the odds of seeing a decision-maker were greatly diminished. Remember now, I'm an old guy, and this was in the old days. Unlike today, almost no businesses, retail or otherwise, were open on Sundays. Obviously, that was not a day to go cold calling. But what if I could speak to seven or eight business owners on Saturdays, even if it was only half as many as I could speak to on the other five workdays of the week? And what if I skipped lunch each day and could speak to an additional prospect or two that hour?

Skipping lunch meant I was making two more sales presentations per day than other salespeople. That's ten more per week. Add the extra seven or eight decision-makers I made sales presentations to on Saturdays, and I'm ahead of everybody else by eighteen prospects who might say yes.

Obviously, I was not the most experienced, and I can assure you, not the most articulate, the most polished, or the most talented sales-person on that list of a hundred. But my revenue results ranking me number one had just about everybody thinking I was. They didn't know I was working harder. The best salesperson, no matter how effective, couldn't beat me when he or she was making eighteen less presentations per week than I. Compared to my four-week results, even the superstar salesperson in Nashville who would report to me went from a hotshot to a "hotnot."

Actually, I exceeded the number of presentations others were making by more than eighteen per week. And I did it by working just half days. That's twelve hours! I started my sales day a lot earlier than any-one else. Picture this. It's 5:20 a.m. I'm sitting on the sidewalk right in front of the door to a hardware store. My back is leaning against that door so when the owner comes to unlock at 5:30, he can't do so without engaging me. I've got a bag of doughnuts and a couple of cups full of hot chocolate to help me make the engagement pretty pleasant. I explain to the owner that he would not meet with me when I called on him the last three days in a row. I tell him one of his employees informed me that he came to work an hour and a half earlier than the store opened so he could catch up on mail and do a little filing before customers showed up. I said he'd regret losing an opportunity to attract more customers if he didn't hear me out while enjoying doughnuts and hot chocolate. He listened. He learned. He bought. He said he couldn't resist a fellow who felt so strongly about the service he was selling that he would get up at 0–dark-thirty to share it.

By the way, no one knew my number-one ranking for four weeks in a row occurred partly because I was working on Saturdays. Since the company's guidelines ended each week on a Friday, I dated all my Saturday sales agreements the two prior days, Thursday and Friday. What I was really doing by making extra sales calls was following a three-word principle practiced by a fellow I'll tell you about here. He started life as an orphan and ended up as a millionaire.

The town and county it was in were rural and small. When the owner of the largest employer in the county retired, almost all the population turned out for a celebration in his honor. It was held in the gymnasium of the local school. A reporter with the weekly newspaper asked the retiring owner if he would step away from the crowd for a minute for an interview. The retiring owner agreed.

The reporter asked, "How have you done so well? We all know you had no mother or father to guide and encourage you, yet you have become a millionaire. Please share with our readers the secret of your success." He responded by saying, "I can sum up the secret of my success in just three little words. They are: *and then some.*"

The reporter had a puzzled look on his face, so the retiring owner explained. "When I was this little 6-year-old living in the orphanage, each day as I walked from the orphan home to my firstgrade class at the local grammar school and then back to the orphanage after school, I would pass by the business from which I am now retiring. One day the owner came out and asked me if I would like a job each day after I finished school. I'm not sure if he really needed help or he just felt sorry for me. In any case, the job was emptying trash cans from all the offices. I emptied the trash cans *and then some*. I wasn't paid to dust each desk, but I did that on top of emptying trash cans. As I got older and stronger, I was given the job of cleaning the toilets throughout the building. I did that *and then some*. I wasn't paid to also mop the bathroom floors, but I did that too.

After I finished high school, I was hired full time. My first job was to separate the shirts we manufactured into stacks of small, medium and large. I did that all day *and then some*. At the end of the day when everyone else had gone home and my shift was over, I took every stack of shirts I had separated during the day and placed them in boxes which I then placed on the shipping docks. Instead of someone having to box shirts and carry them to the docks the next morning, the shirts were already there. That allowed dock workers to immediately begin to load the trucks. I wasn't paid to box shirts and carry them to the loading docks, but I was happy to see that delivery times were shortened as a result of my extra effort."

The explanation continued.

"I was given higher level jobs over the years. I performed all my responsibilities as the job descriptions outlined *and then some*. I was not paid extra for going beyond what was called for in the job descriptions. After many years of doing what was expected of me *and then some*, the owner of the company died. It was a shocking surprise, but in his will the owner explained that because he had no living kin, he was leaving his company to me. He said I had done more to bring him success than anyone else and as a reward, and in appreciation, he wanted to leave the company to me.

As the new owner, I did everything expected of the head of a company *and then some*. Our profits grew and I invested them in more factories. We not only grew throughout the United States but throughout the world. So, those three little words, *and then some*, enabled me to enjoy the successes we are celebrating at this party. That's the simple secret of my success."

Some will dismiss the above story as a fairytale. Some will argue that they don't work hard; they work smart. On top of the fact that it alone won't help you do the best you can't, there are three problems with the "work smart, not hard," philosophy.

First, it presupposes that a person cannot or is not doing both, working smart and working hard simultaneously. If everyone is equally smart, equally well trained, and has all the same latest, most modern and advanced tools with which to work, who will achieve the most? It will be the person that does not rely on smarts alone. It will be the smart person who outworks all the other smart persons.

The second problem with the "work smart, not hard" philosophy is that it's almost impossible to know how much smarter a person needs to work to overcome the extra effort exerted by someone who is working harder. Does a person need to work 10 percent smarter or 100 percent smarter to overcome someone with an approach akin to the *and then some* philosophy? I'm sure most of the other ninety-nine salespeople at our specialty advertising company were smarter—meaning higher IQ, better trained, more experienced, more knowledgeable, and smoother at articulating our sales script—than I. However, their smarts were not so super superior to mine that they could overcome the extra eighteen to twenty sales calls I made each week. Maybe their smarts would have kept me out of first place if I had exceeded their efforts by no more than three or four sales calls each week. But not eighteen to twenty.

The third problem with the "work smart, not hard" philosophy is that it discourages people with limited resources from even trying to compete. The message to people with a lower IQ, less financing, less training, less formal education, less experience, less encouragement, less sophistication, less backing, less machinery, less equipment, less contacts, less vision is: "Don't waste your time. Don't even try. You don't have a chance. You can't beat the big boys and girls. There's already too much competition. You'll never make it."

If a person has got to be smarter, have more cunning, more brains and other resources than others before attempting an undertaking, then competing would be futile and would cease. Without competitors, even those that are inferior, every business would be a monopoly. Every politician would stay in office until death do us part. Every elite athlete would perform by herself or himself.

If someone has to have the same or better brainpower than the smarter, more experienced competitor to have a chance to beat that competitor, there is no motivation to do the best you can't. I've engaged in extra effort all my life because it helped me do what I could not otherwise do with my limited brainpower and other inferior resources. My hard work helped me overcome competitors who were smarter than I.

By the way, if I can't beat the smarter, more experienced person, what's wrong with being almost as good? Almost as successful? If a person's business makes a million dollars, what's wrong if my business makes only a half-million dollars? If a person has never run a business, held political office, jogged a mile, enrolled in college, bought a home, or engaged in any other activity that smarter people have, why can't that person, through hard work, end up with success at least somewhat similar to what the "work smarter, not harder" person has experienced? Who cares if their business is not as profitable, their campaign is not for the White House, their home is not as elegant, their mile run is slower, or their educational experience is not as edifying? They don't have to be the smartest cookie in the jar to succeed. Hard work can compensate for almost any cerebral shortcomings.

Sometimes the person who says, "I work smart, not hard," is merely making an excuse for a lack of drive, determination, passion, energy, and competitiveness. I'm not sure why they do that when it's okay if a person is satisfied with the status quo. I don't have a problem with someone who does not want to be the biggest, the best, the richest, the strongest, the fastest, the firstest with the mostest.

Not everyone has to be a trailblazer. Not everyone has to be motivated to move mountains or do something no one else has ever done. Not everyone has to be the captain of the team, the valedictorian of the class, an Eagle Scout, the president of the company, the star of the show. Not everyone has to be superior at something.

Some can be satisfied with a leisurely, "come what may" approach to life. They have a right to choose to be average. I'm not into changing them, as long as they are being themselves and are happy about it. Those people should just be honest about their priorities and admit they are not interested in going the extra mile to get ahead. They don't need to make the excuse that they work smart, not hard.

Now, if you are reading this book, you are not likely looking for leisure. You desire to overcome obstacles, prove a point, conquer a challenge, initiate the impossible, make a mark, outrageously outperform, do what hasn't been done, triumph over trouble, prevail over problems, handle a handicap, reach a record, hit a high, finish in front, beat the best. You want to do the best you can't.

The above being the case, you need to avoid another oft-repeated excuse for not expending extra energy and effort. This excuse carries a moral or fairness tone with it. It's actually difficult to argue against. It sounds so sensible. Really reasonable. This excuse for not working hard revolves around the desire to lead a balanced life. Now, who can argue against a balanced life? Who can argue against spending an appropriate amount of time with one's family?

The problem is, many who claim they want to lead a balanced life don't act like they do. Yeah, they say they eschew a twelve-hour workday because some things are far more important than climbing the corporate ladder. But when they get home from their shorter workday, they oftentimes watch television instead of reading a book to their kids. Instead of talking with their spouse or kids, they are reading the newspaper while at the dinner table. On Saturday, they are playing golf or tennis rather than taking the kids to the zoo. On Sunday, they are glued to the football broadcast instead of helping the kids with school assignments that must be finished by Monday morning.

I've learned that if you plan your priorities, and if you are willing to forego some personal preferences, you can invest twelve hours a day in your work, community, and other goals and still spend quality and quantity time with your family. You may have to give up golf or tennis on the weekends. Better than giving it up, have your spouse and kids participate with you. Maybe you show your kids you value them by making a seven-minute phone call to them at 3:30 every afternoon of every workday to ask about their school day. Maybe you should schedule a sit-down game like checkers or Monopoly every other Saturday night with your family and never miss it, lest your family think you don't care. You need to prioritize other activities and schedule times to carry them out, so your routine allows hard work but still includes family, recreation, and other important matters. It just takes planning. If you want to be really effective at the planning process, it may help you to go back and reread the chapter titled "You Gotta Predict the Future."

Yes, you may have to sacrifice the boob tube, beers with buddies, and other things that are not especially important, but you can practice the *and then some* philosophy toward your effort at doing the best you can't without a total imbalance toward other important matters.

A good example of this may be A. D. "Pete" Correll. As CEO of Georgia-Pacific Corporation, Pete led that business behemoth's revenue growth from $12 billion when he was first named its head, to $20 billion. Later, he negotiated the company's sale to Koch for $21 billion. In spite of his lofty leadership load with its demand for far more than forty-hour weeks, Pete balanced his life to include giving back to the Atlanta community he called home. He never gave up. He never gave in. He always gave back.

Pete chaired an effort to save Grady Memorial Hospital, Atlanta's public hospital serving the socioeconomically disadvantaged, from bankruptcy or insolvency. He raised $325 million and restructured management, along with enhancing the health-care services the hospital offered. He shared his secret to success in a talk he gave to students at Kennesaw State University. He said, "I had always had a very simple premise in my life that I might not be smarter than anybody else, but I can outwork anybody." On another occasion, he said, "I can get more done in twelve hours than most people can in eight." Pete is proof that hard work can beat smart work while still allowing time for a balanced life that includes the interests of others.

One of the reasons that AssuranceAmerica, the company I cofounded, grew at a faster pace than almost all our competitors was because we spent 20 percent more time in the field making sales visits than did our competition. We sold automobile insurance through independent insurance agencies located in small and large cities in a multistate area. We employed territory managers who traveled to those agencies to educate them about our insurance policies and to motivate them to first consider AssuranceAmerica when considering the multiple companies for which they could write policies.

Competing insurance companies also employ territory managers. Almost 100 percent of competitors gave their territory managers one administrative day out of the five-day workweek to stay at home and catch up on paperwork. It's a day to complete reports, send headquarters information updates, and communicate by phone with people they may not have been able to see during the four days of the week they were in the field.

There was one day each week when I must have been hated by our territory managers. That's the administrative day they would have taken if I had allowed it. I didn't. I wanted them selling five days a week. They thought I was a bit demanding. Demanding, I was. Demeaning, I was not. Territory managers never heard me talk about what they couldn't do. I constantly communicated about what they *could* do. I lauded their efforts. I reminded them of their strengths. I gave constant encouragement. But I wanted them to know that sometimes, the only way to beat bigger, better-known companies was for our territory managers to visit forty agencies per week while competitors were visiting thirty-two.

I told them they had time to do paperwork each night they were on the road holed up in a hotel. In fact, their reports would be a lot clearer and more accurate because they would be written closer to the time the activity took place. I suggested that if they had not completed reports by Friday night, that they should get up at five a.m. on Saturday morning and work three hours to finish them. That meant they took away no family time, as nobody else would be up that early. At eight o'clock, they could wake up their spouses and kids and all enjoy breakfast together while discussing what they might do with one another that weekend. To me, that seemed like a perfect procedure for working hard and enjoying a balanced life at the same time.

On top of the above regimen, I suggested (no mandate here) they do what nobody else, and I mean *nobody* else, was doing in the territory managing/selling world: visit insurance agencies for a half day on one Saturday out of each month. That would amount to an additional thirty-six to forty-eight agency visits per year they'd make over and above what their competitors would make. I even suggested it would be a good way to balance work and family. How could that be? Hey, take your spouses and/or kids with you on that Saturday field trip.

Normally, it would not be professionally proper to have your kids tag along while making a sales or service visit to a client. While that's true, I explained that if you walk into an agency only rarely and tell them you want to show your children and/or spouse what you do to make a living, that agency will gladly accommodate you with a smile. Weeks after your visit, the agency will talk about it. So will your spouse and/or kids who accompanied you. You'll differentiate yourself from your competitors in a very distinct way. Your harder/longer workweek will make such a positive impact that it won't matter how smart, how big, or how technologically advanced your competitors are. You'll beat them.

By the way, I told our territory managers to buy lunch for their spouses and kids as an end-of-work treat on those Saturdays and the company would pay for it. It worked wonderfully well. I know because I occasionally accompanied them on these combined business/family outings, and I observed the dramatically positive impact being made.

If you really want to do the best you can't, you must, literally or figuratively, engage in some Saturday selling. It's the *and then some* principle. It's working harder than others or harder than your old self. I don't know what your *and then some* activity is, but it will give you great advantage if you figure it out.

When I decided to run for the Georgia State Senate when I was thirty-four years old, I had no chance of winning unless I figured out an *and then some* approach. With no experience ever serving in any elected office, no campaign organization, no name recognition, no capability to personally finance a campaign, and no network of contributors to donate funds to cover the expenses of a campaign, I knew my only chance of winning was to outwork everybody else seeking that senate seat.

There were eleven people running—six Democrats and five Republicans. I'd have to win enough votes to get into a runoff, then win the runoff, and then win the general election. I'd have to upstage a couple of wealthy people who were running and could buy attention and name recognition. I'd have to beat a well-known city councilman. I'd need to outpoll an experienced member of the State House of

Representatives. He was very popular in his house district, which was located within the senate district. I would need to reach a population of 150,000 people. The average expenditure for winning a state senate seat was $50,000. This was 1974. Today, it costs almost $500,000 to win. I'd be lucky if I could scrounge up $2,000 by contributing half that amount myself and, hopefully, raising the other half.

Almost everyone told me that my measly molehill of money could not overcome the mighty mountains of money my opponents would spend. It's impossible, they said, for $2,000 to beat $50,000 of smart expenditures for radio, direct mail, and newspaper advertising. But I put into practice what I preach about planning in Chapter 6. Hey, be assured that the advice in this book is not dreamed-up theory. I practiced the principles incorporated herein then, and I practice them now. I believed I could do what others thought was impossible. I would do the best I can't. But I needed a plan, and I needed to put in extra effort executing it.

Knock, knock. Ring, ring. House after house. Door after door. The plan called for me to start at five p.m. on weekdays. Well, the door knocking did. Beforehand, I got up at four o'clock each morning so I could get to work by five. Normally, my work schedule was seven a.m. to seven p.m. I felt an obligation to give my employer the same time and effort I had given before I made the decision to run for the state senate. I also liked my work and didn't want to cut back on something so challenging, enjoyable, and fulfilling. As an aside, let me say here that I've never understood people who, upon hearing about one of my frequent out of town trips, ask if I'm traveling for business or pleasure. My response has always been, "You are asking your question the wrong way. You should ask if I'm traveling for business or leisure, as they are both pleasurable." That why I say my work efforts are more than an obligation. They're a pleasure.

Saturdays' campaign starts wouldn't be earlier than 9:30 a.m. because not everyone would be up until then. The plan also called for more knocking and ringing around 1:30 p.m. on Sundays when most folks were back from church and finished with lunch. Door knocking and bell ringing had to cease at nine p.m. each of those seven days because too many folks were in their pajamas after nine.

I'll confess here that one night when I walked up to a house a couple of minutes before nine, I threw my opponent under the bus. After ringing the doorbell at this home in a middle-class subdivision, I heard a mean-sounding shout that asked, "What are you doing ringing my bell so late at night?" I replied, "Sir, I'm here to personally ask for your vote in the upcoming state senate election." He responded, "I'd never vote for anyone rude enough to disturb my family this late at night. What's your name?" The whole time I was campaigning, I tried to never disparage my opponents. I really believe campaigns should be positive and issue oriented, not personal. But on this occasion, the devil made me do it. I answered the man's question by saying, "Marion Mundy." He was a city councilman who had gotten into the runoff election with me. He had a memorable slogan: "Vote for Mundy on Tuesday." Well, I know for sure one vote he didn't get on Tuesday.

In any case, all this door-to-door activity took place no matter how cold the winter or how hot the summer. Those terrible thunderstorms didn't deter me, because I carried a plastic umbrella with no metal pieces to attract a lightning strike. I didn't let wasp nests above doors, spiderwebs across entrances, or growling dogs deter me. I was a man on a mission.

People were used to state senate campaigns that started, at most, maybe ninety days before election day. Early in the campaign, I informed each voter on whose door I knocked that I had to start a full year before the primary vote would take place because constituents wouldn't know me or what I stood for if I did not personally meet them and ask for their votes. I explained that that was because there would not be one penny spent on advertising. There would be no money for mailings. My only means of reaching out for supporters was to start campaigning early enough to enable me to walk 100 percent of my district and personally ask for votes.

Of course, with the little money I had, I had to print a brochure that outlined what I stood for. I printed enough to give to each and every voter household. The only other item in my budget, except extra expenses for shoe leather, was yard signs. At each door I knocked, I said that I thought it was wrong for candidates to nail campaign signs to trees or stake them on public property beside streets and highways. That was illegal. And even though I could get away with doing it because the laws against it were not strictly enforced, I felt it was hypocritical to aspire to be a lawmaker while being a lawbreaker. Thus, I said I would put up no illegal signs, and I asked at each door I knocked if I could put a campaign sign in their yard. I would place it exactly three weeks before the election. Win or lose, I promised to take it down no later than two days after the election. After hearing my story about a personal door-knocking campaign without any advertising other than yard signs, a significant number of households I visited agreed to sign a form giving me written permission to advertise in their yards.

If I had planned properly and calculated correctly, I knew I could cover the whole 150,000 population area over a twelve-month period of time. I did as planned because I was relentless in spending time and energy while others were spending something else: money. Twenty-five times my mere $2,000. And when my volunteers with their car trunks and pickup beds full of yard signs staked them out exactly three weeks before the election, it looked like a groundswell of support had happened overnight.

Of course, it took a year of sweat to generate a night of sensation. Until that time, almost no candidates had had a sustained door-knocking campaign. It is much more prevalent today. But even now, many campaigns hire people to knock on doors and ask for votes for the candidate they represent. Some may believe that's smart. But believe me, that kind of smart won't beat the personal effort and hard work of one individual who has an *and then some* approach.

For those reading this who are not familiar with Georgia politics, you may be interested to know that serving as a state senator in Georgia is not a full-time, full-pay job. Just like their constituents, state senators have to make a living throughout the year. The senate meets to consider laws for forty days spread from early January to mid-April each year. On those days, I also had to live by the *and then some* principle. My alarm would go off at three a.m. so I could go to my office at work before heading to the state capitol at eight or nine. Then I'd head back to my work office at four or five in the afternoon so I could earn a living for my family. The terms are for two years. There are committee meetings and constituent meetings throughout the year. Thus, hard work does not end after the general election is over. Hard work must continue, but serving is so satisfying that it's worth the *and then some* scenario that is necessary in serving your company and your constituents.

Now, whether you want to do the best you can't in business, politics, jogging, family relationships, neighborliness, educational pursuits, debt control, healthy living, or anything else that may seem impossible, you must first determine what hard work and effort you are willing to invest. That's necessary because you will almost always do the best you can't only when you do what you or others normally do *and then some.*

For Leo, a seller of newspapers on a street corner in Philadelphia, it was wearing a tuxedo with tails and a top hat. All others who were hawking newspapers on street corners for the *Philadelphia Inquirer* did the expected. They wore jeans and T-shirts. Since newsprint ink messes up the hands and clothes of anyone handling newspapers, jeans and T-shirts seem reasonable. Because Leo went beyond the reasonable or the expected, customers drove or walked three or four blocks out of their way to buy their newspapers from him. His "do the reasonable *and then some*" approach enabled Leo to sell three times more newspapers each day than anyone else.

The chance of being chosen to fill the part-time job after school each day was a long shot for anyone. The economy was in recession. Unemployment for any segment of society, much less students, was sky high. The line at the application desk stretched out the door and wound its way around three blocks. Because she walked away from her place as the last person in line, it looked like she wasn't willing or able to invest the hours it would take to reach the employment office. But wait, maybe she hadn't given up after all. After a little while, she again took the last spot. Hours later, she got the job. She had left the line to visit a courier service, which she paid to deliver a message to the employer. It said, "Please don't hire anybody until you talk to the little girl with pigtails and the polka-dot dress in the back of the line." She got the job because she waited in line like everybody else *and then some.*

Like the doctor at the teaching hospital, the *and then some* approach will not only help you achieve the end result you seek; it may well offer you another benefit at the end of the day. He was so good at his profession that medical students learned by watching him perform surgery while they were behind viewing windows. After he finished each operation and the patient was wheeled to a recovery room, the doctor would take questions from the students. One student remarked, "Doctor, we have been taught in all our classes that at the end of surgery, only one properly tied knot is required to secure the suture. But I noticed you tied two knots. Why is that?"

The doctor replied, "That's what I call my sleeping knot. You see, after an operation is over and I've gone home for the evening and eventually go to bed and fall asleep, without fail, I'll wake up at one or two a.m. with a burning question on my mind. That question means life or death to my patient because if I don't have the right answer, the patient could bleed to death. I ask myself, did I properly tie a knot at the end of the suture? Then I remember that I not only properly tied one knot; I properly tied two knots at the end. Remembering that, I snuggle my head back on my pillow and immediately go back to sleep for a peaceful and restful night. That's why I call it my sleeping knot."

Practice the *and then some* principle and you will not only do the best you can't—you will sleep well too!

CHAPTER 8

OLD DOGS/PEOPLE MUST LEARN NEW TRICKS

*How to Skin a Rattlesnake, Dance a
Jig, Calm an Irate Customer*

In 1963, RIGHT AFTER PRINCE Edward County, Virginia, decided that in order to avoid integration, it would no longer provide public schools, Robert Kennedy, then attorney general of the United States, spoke at the Kentucky Centennial Celebration of the Emancipation Proclamation. He said:

"We may observe with much sadness and irony that outside of Africa, south of the Sahara, where education is still a difficult challenge, the only places on earth known not to provide public education are Communist China, North Vietnam, Sarawak, Singapore, British Honduras—and Prince Edward County, Virginia. Something must be done about Prince Edward County."

Now, sixty years later, thank goodness, such morally deficient decisions regarding race and education have long ago been corrected.

However, there is still a widespread wasteland where learning opportunities are overlooked, rejected, or ignored. Where that is the case, whether with companies or with individuals, the chances of anyone doing the best she or he can't is almost nonexistent. Thus, my advice if you are not constantly learning and teaching new tricks is: you've got to do something about that.

When I was CEO of AssuranceAmerica, a risk-bearing insurance company that sells our policies through thousands of independent insurance agencies, I felt privileged to visit those agencies to determine how our company could better serve them. I would frequently hear agency owners say there was really nothing I could do to solve their biggest problem—because their biggest problem had nothing to do with any shortcomings of AssuranceAmerica.

What was their problem? I'd hear agency owner after agency owner say they would get enough telephone calls asking for price quotes on automobile insurance that if they could get just half the callers to come in and buy, their agencies would be, if not on fire, at least somewhat smoldering in sales. They lamented that perhaps only 25 percent of callers subsequently came in to buy. If they could double that to 50 percent, what a welcomed win that would be. Even though they were right to say AssuranceAmerica was not the problem, they were wrong to say we (or they) could not supply the solution.

I'd tell insurance agency owners, if you want your customer service representatives (CSRs) to motivate more telephone callers to actually visit your agency, they can do it. Oh, yes, there's a way to become effective at getting a higher percentage of callers to come to the agency to buy a policy. There's a way for an agent to calm an irate customer. There's a way to sell an additional product, such as roadside service or accidental death and disability coverage (AD&D), on top of the basic automobile policy an agency sells its customers. The way? Learn how to do all the above.

You want to wrestle an alligator without becoming its supper? Have someone teach you. You want to skin a rattlesnake? The answer, other than very carefully, is have someone teach you. How do you dance a jig, fly a hot-air balloon, land a helicopter, cook a peach pie, extract tonsils, or do a better job of growing and managing an insurance agency? All these things take training. Someone must teach you.

The very fact that an agency owner's CSRs can legally sell insurance in the first place is because someone trained them until they learned enough to pass a qualifying exam. CSRs could learn to prepare agencies' tax returns if someone taught them to do so. CSRs could learn to sell life insurance in addition to automobile insurance if someone taught them. CSRs could literally learn to skin a rattlesnake if someone taught them that skill.

If you are an owner or manager of a company, large or small, there are a lot of things you can do to those who work for you. You can cajole them, bully them, intimidate them, shame them, bore them, ignore them, harass them, or fire them. Instead, why not teach them, educate them, strengthen them, build them, improve them, train them, promote them?

Jack Welch, GE's former chairman and CEO who was so revered, devoted 30 percent of his time to leadership development. He even personally taught once a week at GE's executive training institute. Noel Tichy, who was a professor at the University of Michigan's Business School, said, "Great leaders have to be great teachers." And regarding Jack Welch, he said, "That's where he gets his leverage."

In suggesting to insurance agency owners that the solution to motivating more callers to actually come into their offices and buy a policy was/is teaching CSRs how to do it, I acknowledged that not all agency owners are great teachers. That fact, along with the excuse that small insurance agencies, unlike GE, are not large enough to provide the degree of formal training GE provides caused some owners to rate my recommendations as unrealistic, irrelevant rants.

I'd have to convince them there were/are some pretty practical ways to train themselves and their associates, even if they employed only one CSR. I'd ask if they really, really wanted their agency to have a better future. When the reply was in the affirmative, as it always was, then I'd say, "The future starts right now. You can let your associates stay stuck in the status quo, drift, remain empty, be immobile, and continue to wallow in the misery of mediocrity by letting them repetitively perform the same tomorrow as they do today. Or you can help them achieve a tomorrow they have not yet imagined because you taught them today.

My advice to small one- or two-person agencies was to start by going to the bookstore and buying a book for each employee. Ask them to read the book and highlight any particularly meaningful or valuable sentences or paragraphs. Tell them to write notes in the book's margins if they have a thought or question about that part of the book. Tell them the book is theirs to keep, so mark it up if that enhances the learning process. Then, once a month or maybe even once every two weeks, review a chapter or two or three of the book together at the agency one hour before opening to the public. Bring in coffee and egg biscuits and pay the associates for the extra hour they are investing. In the long run, it won't cost the owner anything because the associate will be so much more effective than before the training took place.

Discuss the book. Learn from it. Practice what is learned. Each month or each quarter, choose another book. Better yet, let the associate choose a subject in which he or she is interested. Do this all year long. My message was, start today! If you do, your associates will have a stronger and more effective tomorrow. And your agency will learn more, know more, and perform better than the competitor down the street or across town that does zero training.

Books on selling by phone, selling in person, answering objections, time management, organizational skills, human relations, ethics, customer service, and a host of other subjects will strengthen an insurance agency or any other business way beyond the price of the materials. What associates couldn't do yesterday can become accomplished attributes of associates tomorrow because an owner or manager cared enough to teach them today.

Regardless of whether you are an owner or an employee of a business, and whether your company does or does not provide learning opportunities, you don't have to wait for someone to provide you learning opportunities. On your own, you can and should be a lifelong learner. In fact, if you are not enhancing learning, you are not enhancing earning. A study by the US Department of Labor reported that businesspeople who read seven or more business books per year earn 230 percent more income than people who read just one book per year.

In another study, this one from 5,280 people from Austria, Belgium, the Czech Republic, Denmark, France, Germany, Italy, Sweden, and the Netherlands, it was found that those who read at least ten noncompulsory schoolbooks per year ended up with 21 percent more income. If you were told that all you had to do is read ten books over the next twelve months in order to make $60,500 instead of $50,000, or $121,000 instead of $100,000, wouldn't you visit Barnes & Noble, Amazon, or your public library without delay? Then don't delay.

If reading more leads to earning more, doesn't that principle mean you excel at a greater degree than you otherwise would, whether your reading involves business practices, family relations, hobbies, or any other pursuits or activities? You'll grow a better garden than I if you read books about how to do it and I do not. You'll make better pottery than I if you read books about how to do it and I do not.

Reading books on the right subject matter can help you identify bird species or the kind of trees growing in your yard. Reading the right books can teach you how to better race motorcycles if you want to compete in that sport. Books can help you prevail at speaking in public, laying concrete, writing condolence letters, framing pictures, handling personnel problems, maintaining healthy exercise and eating habits, managing sales, managing money, budgeting, and a long list of other things. So if you want to be more skilled, knowledgeable, and prepared than those who don't read, what must you do? Learn to read. Read to learn.

CEOs of major enterprises are reported to read an average of one book per week. The US Bureau of Labor Statistics says people working for these CEOs will average one book per year. How'd you like to be in the top one percent of readers of books? That task is probably not as strenuous and stunningly scary as it sounds. You certainly don't have to emulate executives who read one book per week. All you have to do is read one book per month to leave behind 99 percent of other people.

If you are interviewing for a job, won't you likely display more knowledge if you have read twelve12 business books during the prior year? Everything else being equal between you and other candidates, won't you have a better chance of being hired if you have read twelve books over the past year and they have read one? If you are having a conversation at a cocktail party, aren't you more likely to be more enlightening and even more entertaining if you've read twelve books in the last year and others in the conversation have read only one?

Talk to me five years from now and I will have read one hundred books. Will you have soaked up as much information as I will over that same period of time? If we are competing for a job and my reading has focused on business subjects, you will be at a distinct disadvantage if you are among the 99 percent who will have read only five books over five years.

Now, you have a choice. You can possess the same amount of knowledge and be the same old person five years from now as you are today.

Or you can grow and be better informed and more capable than you are today. But you are not going to attain personal growth by accident. Reaching your potential won't be happenstance. To reach full potential, it must be purposefully planned. That's how I know I will read one hundred books over the next five years, just as I read a hundred books over the past five years. I've had a plan for several years. Just as I might set an appointment with my dentist, I set an appointment with my book. Thank goodness, the dental appointments are less frequent than my book appointments. My book appointments are also less expensive than my dental appointments—and a whole lot more fun, too.

It's not easy for me. When I read a book, I've really done the best I can't. You see, a few years ago, I came to the realization that I needed to regularly read books if I was going to have an edge, an advantage, and advance in business—really in life as a whole. I had not been reading very much because I failed every time I sat down to read a book. I have had attention deficit hyperactivity disorder (ADHD) since I was a child. It adversely affected my ability to read because I couldn't concentrate. I'd start a book and realize thirty or forty minutes later that my mind was working overtime and wandering waywardly. As a result, I would have advanced no further than eight or ten pages. Without realizing it, I had been daydreaming for a longer period of time than I had been reading. So I came up with a plan. I couldn't read a book in one or two sittings. But I could concentrate long enough to read twenty pages per day. That's one hundred pages if I read Monday through Friday. That's four hundred pages per month. Assuming an average book has 240 pages, that's 1.67 books per month. That's twenty books per year.

Before I retired, I'd get to the office an hour or so before anyone else. My first priority was to read twenty pages before my phone started ringing or people would begin to stop by my office. I would not compromise my reading schedule. When I wasn't going to the office, I read twenty pages while on my elliptical machine, which I use for my daily three-mile jog. I can't read on a treadmill because I'm making a pounding motion that makes words too "bouncy." The elliptical machine is a smooth motion that doesn't make the words blurry.

It should be obvious from the above that the kind of learning I'm suggesting has nothing to do with a college education. While I believe a bachelor's, master's, or doctorate degree is valuable, I don't think a university is universally useful. There are lots of people who drop out of school but end up successful. That's because they never quit learning.

Yes, some super-successful people don't have a college degree. However, they are prolific readers. Bill Gates, the multibillionaire founder of Microsoft, fits that category. He dropped out of college but continues to learn by reading some fifty books per year. It's his approach to reading that I recommend to those who are perusing these pages. He's not trying to set a record for the number of books he's read. He's reading to learn. He's reading for education, not entertainment.

Because Gates' fame and fortune are so far from the world in which I fit, it's surprising, but he and I treat books in somewhat the same fashion. I write notes in the margins of books I read. I may write that I strongly agree or strongly disagree with this or that sentence I've underlined. I may tell myself to call so-and-so and ask what that person's thoughts are about this or that paragraph. I may ask a manager in my company about implementing an idea expounded upon in the book I'm reading. I highlight with red or yellow what I consider the meat of the matter so I can flip through the book at a later date and easily see and be reminded of the important points.

In an article in *Ladders*, written by C. W. Headley on March 17, 2021, Gates explained his approach when he is quoted as saying, "For me, taking notes helps make sure that I'm really thinking hard about what's in there." Again, it's a quest for education, not entertainment. In this same article, Gates is quoted again. He said, "You don't really get old until you stop reading." In my opinion, he's right. Whatever your age, reading can broaden knowledge, expand vision, alter approaches, refresh outlook, change opinions, and chart new paths. All that, even if you are a hundred years old!

Bill Gates may be a good example of how lifelong learning helps someone do the best he can't. However, he's a poor example if it leaves the impression that continuous learning gained through reading is only for those with a high IQ who are among the rich and famous. Reading and learning can be proportionately just as important to the career of a janitor with average intelligence and no more than a ninth-grade education. If such a janitor wants to do the best he can't, reading may be one of the means by which he does so. He is not doomed to a destiny of doing only what he is doing today. His tomorrow can be transformed by what he reads today.

If through reading, he discovers a more environmentally friendly formula for polishing floors, that's likely to stand him in stronger stead with management than his peers who use more contaminating compounds. Maybe reading teaches him not only how to fire up and clean furnaces, but also how to repair them. Maybe through reading, he learns inventory-control processes that make maintaining adequate supplies of cleaning fluids, equipment, and material less costly. His career can continue on cruise control or can race rapidly ahead. But getting ahead requires gaining something in his head.

So, whether you are the CEO of Microsoft or the janitor, lifelong learning is essential if you don't want to stay stuck in the status quo. If you agree with that, then you must discipline yourself to read. You must come up with a plan that works for you and then stick with it. Regularly reading books about your work, your hobby, or other pursuits for which you possess passion will help change you from who you are to who you want to be. It will help you be better than you are right now. It will help you do the best you can't.

Many of us have had to form positive reading habits after we reached adulthood. It's easier if we get into the reading habit earlier. If you have kids, help them create a love of learning and a belief in books while they are really young. Our society has done a poor job of that. The Bureau of Labor Statistics says that a typical teen enjoys five hours of leisure time each day. Adults that were surveyed thought teens should spend an hour and fifteen minutes of that leisure time each day researching and reading. But teens spend, on average, only six minutes of each day browsing books. As Attorney General Kennedy might say, surely something should be done about that.

Now, reading books is not the only way to learn and grow to the point that you are capable of doing the best you can't. Following are three approaches I've taken in business to ensure we had a chance of doing better than I could have otherwise led my companies to do. These principles can also be applied to personal pursuits.

Two Vital Characteristic New Hires Must Have

Too often, in the hiring process, "A" people hire "B" people who hire "C" people. That formula guarantees regression, not progression. At best, it leads to an enterprise that can do what it can but isn't capable of doing what it can't. I've always tried to hire people who report to me that are stronger than I. An argument I've heard against that is that, if the new hire is stronger than I am, I may have to pay the person more than I make. So, what's the problem with that?

Thinking that a "second in command" must be paid less than the "first in command" may well set in motion a downward spiral in intellect, energy, vision, innovativeness, and know-how. Considering that considerable cost, it's a better bargain to boost the new hire's billfold beyond your own. Plus, stronger people don't kick you out. They kick you up. As a result, your promotion will produce a paycheck that will soon surpass the new hire's paycheck.

There are a lot of positive characteristics I seek in these stronger people who report to me. Two are so essential that no prospect will be invited to join my team without them.

One: my direct reports have to be smarter than I am (I know; I know; that's easy). Here's why they need to be smarter than I. Pitfalls in my plans may not be plain to me. I've had some pretty crazy ideas in my time. I want someone who is smart enough to know when my plans aren't so positive. I want someone who knows when I'm crazy and about to mess up a project or wreck the company. If my direct reports aren't smarter than I, how will they steer me from stupidity or, on the other hand, guide me to greatness? Thus, I'm looking for a head on the hire's shoulders. My direct reports need to have big, brilliant brainpower to help me solve problems, seize potential, and do the best I can't.

The second essential characteristic I require of my direct reports involves a part of the body that's connected to the brain. That's the backbone. You see, if someone is smart enough to know when I'm crazy but is so spineless she or he can't say so, their brain is of no benefit. That's because a company's methods are not the main thing that will determine how well it performs. It is its mindset. Therefore, it's crucial to have direct reports who have the courage to express critical, contrarian concerns today. The resulting discomfort created early on will keep a present problem from becoming a major catastrophe tomorrow and further into the future. I don't know if there really is an abominable snowman in the Himalayan Mountains, as some say. I do know there needs to be an abominable no man (or woman) in my company to keep me from carrying out some of my craziness.

Right here, I feel the need to share information about two people whose brains and backbones helped me do the best I can't in business. They, along with lots of other terrifically talented people, helped me grow an insurance company from zero to $200 million in premium in just ten years. In describing these two people, I may help you define the kind of person you should hire next time you are looking for a direct report.

When I became president and CEO of AssuranceAmerica Corporation, it had zero sales and employed zero people other than me. It started as an independent insurance agency that would grow into a chain of fifty locations in three states. Later, we formed a subsidiary whose operation provided products (automobile insurance policies) to sell through our fifty agencies. Then we worked to appoint another two thousand-plus agencies we did not own to sell our policies to their customers. Long before we reached the size I just described, I knew I needed day-to-day help.

At the time I got into the automobile insurance profession, I was already a somewhat seasoned, mature, experienced executive in the business world. I had been vice president and general manager of two subsidiaries of a small but fast-growing entrepreneurial operation that over a few short years became a large operation listed on the New York Stock Exchange (NYSE). Long before it reached that size, I left that company and went into business for myself. With the help of a lot of good people, my company grew and grew. We ended up expanding our service into several states. Thus, I knew a little about sales, marketing, budgeting, profit and loss statements, and managing finance, operations, administration, and people. However, I did not know beans about insurance. But I got into the business after some in-depth research about a specialized area of automobile insurance that I thought would be a fast-growing, profitable profession to pursue. My lack of insurance experience—my ignorance—meant I needed to recruit and hire Joe.

Joe Skruck was what I wasn't. Knowing he was stronger than I and that he knew a hundred times more about insurance than I, I brought him into AssuranceAmerica as executive vice president (EVP). I told Joe I was getting old and would retire and give him my job within eight to ten years if his performance merited it. Did it ever!

Insurance done right must have a large analytic and statistical element that I could not provide. Joe could. Fraud must be ferreted out of the claims-paying process, or the result is failure. I did not know that process. Joe did. I had no experience to help me understand the intricacies of rate segmentation, actuarial forecasts, or risk assessment. Joe did.

On top of all the above, Joe had previously been a part of a larger company, whereas my experience was with mostly smaller entrepreneurial enterprises. He understood that as our company became larger, it needed to employ some professional management tools and techniques. He helped us install some processes, procedures, and solid systems that weren't run by seat of the britches, spur of the moment guesswork. He provided the right mixture of entrepreneurial and professional management. That meant his professional management approach did not saddle our company with the kind of bureaucratic baggage some large outfits carry.

Joe is my proof that when you hire someone stronger than yourself, you can reach goals that others think are impossible. Joe, in turn, has hired people strong enough to take the company to an even higher level after Joe is gone. Indeed, because of that, our company will continue to do the best it can't!

Guy Millner deserves more credit for my success in business than does anyone else. He possesses the two characteristics I noted are essential in those who report to me. He certainly has a more brilliant brain than I, and he has never been reluctant to tell me when he thinks I am crazy. However, he has never reported to me. Guy and I were cofounders of AssuranceAmerica. In its early days, he was the passive financier of the company I was attempting to grow and manage day to day as CEO. Today, he leads the company as executive chairman.

Even though some would say Guy's substantial financial investment in AssuranceAmerica and his role as cofounder and chairman gave him the right to call me crazy anytime he saw me heading in a disastrous direction, I credit him with being direct about it but never unprofessional or mean-spirited in word, attitude, or tone. Never did I experience harshness, temper tantrums, or uncontrolled emotional outbursts from him when he disagreed with what I had done or what I wanted to do—not even in the early days, when our company was losing money.

I partnered with Guy, not only because he was smarter than I and willing to tell me when I was tilting toward trouble, but because I knew he could grow an acorn into an oak tree. He had done it before. After working his way through Florida State University selling pots and pans door to door, he migrated to Atlanta and started a two-person personnel agency. Under his leadership, it grew to become a $1.4 billion temporary help, contract staffing, and facilities management company with 491 branches nationally and internationally.

A lot of people have big dreams that are nothing more than wishful thinking. Guy had turned dreams into reality. I knew if we teamed up that he could teach me some things I didn't know. What I would learn would stir and stimulate my soul and give me the ability to stretch beyond my prior small successes. I would gain enough from him to do the best I can't.

More important than the strengths and experiences he had that I didn't was his integrity. I know Guy's word is as good as a written contract. Having worked with him over an eight-year period in the early stages of the company that I mentioned above that became a NYSE firm, we had a lot of handshake deals. It would have been a lot less costly for him if he had conveniently forgotten some of those verbal agreements. He didn't. His memory was like an elephant's. Now, that's the kind of person with whom you should partner.

People with a smart head on their shoulders and a strong-as-steel spine running down their backs are probably better at helping you do the best you can't than the book learning to which I gave a boost at the beginning of this chapter. But don't limit yourself to either or. Just think what your stronger self will be able to achieve if you provide yourself the backing of books, brains, and backbones.

Outstanding Outsiders

If, based on the above, you think the only resources to help you succeed beyond your own capabilities are internal resources like Joe or Guy, then you will miss out on a strong supply source that is the mother of all mother lodes. Question: who has knowledge, information, experience, and expertise about your industry or interests? Answer: companies or individuals in the same or similar business you are in. They are not only competitors; they are colleagues. At least, they could be. Unless they are cutting ethical corners, mistreating customers, and giving the industry a bad reputation, competitors are not your enemies. They are your friends.

Have you noticed how automobile dealerships seem to locate their sales and service facilities right next to one another? That's no coincidence. They understand that a good source for customers is right next door at a competing place of business. Maybe the competitor does not have the right car color. Maybe they don't have an attractive financing program. Maybe the competitor's customers walk over to the next door dealer solely out of curiosity. Maybe the competitor's customers wouldn't drive across town to find a better car color or finance plan, but it's convenient to walk next door. It's a win-win for car competitors to congregate on corners across from one another.

Competing airlines are also cooperating airlines. It's profitable for Delta to fly a full load of passengers from Atlanta to New Brunswick. But if half those passengers end their flight in New Brunswick and the other half want to fly on to Amsterdam, it is not profitable for Delta to carry only a half load to Amsterdam. Thus, Delta partners with KLM to cover the last part of the trip for what would have been only 50 percent capacity for Delta. KLM may have a full passenger load from Amsterdam to New Brunswick, but half those passengers end their trip in New Brunswick and half want to continue on to Atlanta. KLM can't make money carrying only a half load of passengers to Atlanta. Thus, they partner with Delta to complete the trip for the Atlanta half of the KLM passenger load. These competitors become colleagues because it's the best way for both to profitably fly passengers.

These and other airlines also share the cost of air traffic controllers. Each airline does not hire its own controllers. They all pay their fair share for a collection of cooperating controllers to guide their respective planes to safe takeoffs and landings. By the way, this cooperation starts well before any planes take off. Airlines also have ticketing systems that are owned and operated by more than one airline. This saves hundreds of millions of dollars each airline would have to spend on developing their own software and automated systems if they didn't split the cost with competitors. Eventually, that lower cost ends up saving consumers from having to pay additional monies for tickets to cover higher overhead of airlines that paid to have their own reservation systems.

There were (are) a lot of good reasons why the insurance company where I was CEO had (has) a far above average claims department. A major reason was because key managers in our claims department and I visited competitors to probe their practices. We spent two to three days on their premises inspecting their operation and questioning their management. We delved into their best practices in hopes of incorporating them into our operation. Was there a parts supplier or a chain of body shops both companies might use to reduce costs through volume purchases? Were they aware of charlatan repair shops we should not recommend to our policyholders? How did they ferret out fake wrecks and false claims so claim dollars were spent only on our honest policyholders who deserve the best possible repair work?

Through these visits, we became aware of a few processes and procedures we would not have known about if we viewed competitors as enemies. We found that some of their practices were better than some of our company's practices. The end result was that we learned to do some things we couldn't otherwise do. We learned to do the best we can't.

Of course, these competitors also visited us to determine our best practices. They learned enough that they would also be able to do some things they could not do before spending a couple of days inspecting our operation. Obviously, neither of us shared any proprietary secrets (not sure we had any). But both benefited by being *with* one another, as opposed to being *wary* of one another.

The principle I'm espousing can be applied to far more areas of life than just business. If you want to know how to better perform in a motorcycle race, who better to learn from than someone who has won more races than you? If you want to enhance your canasta card game, call the best players in town and ask if they will share their expertise with you. If you want to know how to lose weight or how to solicit donations for your favorite charity, determine who has done it and ask them how they did it. If you want to win the next cake-baking contest, talk with someone who has walked off with a blue ribbon or two in the past. You may be pleasantly surprised at how accommodating competitors can be. Many, maybe most, will willingly work with you to help you do what you thought you couldn't do.

Flipping Hamburgers

My phone is ringing. It's an acquaintance of mine who is calling to share some bad news about our mutual friend Archie. Who's Archie? I mentioned him in the chapter of this book that describes my experience as a board member of Faulkner University. Astoundingly talented would be an appropriately accurate description of Archie. He built and manages scores of senior-citizen complexes across the United States. Long before such success, he grew up in a family that couldn't fund his college courses. He had enough basketball skills that an athletic scholarship was his means to an education. He was smart enough that it could have been an academic scholarship. His competitiveness, smarts, and hardworking habits had earned him an incredible income and a high net worth. He used some of his assets to help fund a Christian mission in Honduras. He helped buy farm equipment and build school and medical facilities for the Honduran locals. But, according to the caller on the other end of the phone, Archie was flat broke.

How could my friend Archie be broke and have fallen on hard times and I not know about it? How had the caller gotten such an impression? It turned out that the caller had gone to a McDonald's to get a bite to eat. When he walked in the door, he saw Archie in the back of the store, flipping hamburgers. The caller told me he quickly turned around and exited the store because he knew Archie would be embarrassed to be seen in such dire straits that he had to resort to being a fast-order cook in a McDonald's.

There's a cliché about believing none of what you hear and only half of what you see. Apply it here. Archie wasn't broke. In fact, he had enough money to consider buying a dozen or so McDonald's franchises for his grandkids. However, McDonald's won't sell you franchises unless you first work every job within one of their restaurants. They want to be sure you understand the basics of the business. They want you to have a feel for every facet of the operation. They want you to experience the pleasant and not-so-pleasant parts before you make a decision to buy a franchise. That's why Archie was flipping hamburgers. But, you ask, what does flipping hamburgers have to do with doing the best you can't?

Well, flipping hamburgers exposes you to something with which you have little or no experience. You'll find out if you like or don't like the activity. As an outsider who hasn't had a habit of flipping hamburgers, you may see a way to do it better than an experienced person going through a rote routine who has never questioned whether there is a better way. You may learn a principle that you can apply to other areas of work or life. It dawned on me that Archie's activities at McDonald's were applicable at AssuranceAmerica.

It motivated me to work a half or a whole day or two in almost every department of my company. Figuratively speaking, I'd be flipping hamburgers. Flipping hamburgers translated to my working in the mail room for a day. That led me to ask if it would be more cost effective if we bought better processors and upgraded our automation. Or should we contract with a company that specialized in managing mail facilities? Flipping hamburgers—in this case, you might call it flipping mail—led us to the realization that we could execute our mail function more quickly and less costly than we ever thought we could.

Another area where I figuratively flipped hamburgers was by sitting with a person that took first calls reporting car accidents. Listening in on conversations with our policyholders and our intake person led me to question whether our words, tone of voice, and attitude were as good as they should be. After all, we should be relieving stress from those who needed their cars repaired and claims paid so they could get back to normal life as quickly as possible.

The point is that the view from my executive office did not enable me to envision or experience everything I needed to if our company was to exceed expectations. That little corporate corner was too confining. I needed to flip hamburgers to discover what we were doing well and what we were doing poorly. I wouldn't know what we should be doing, but weren't doing, if I didn't flip hamburgers throughout our operation.

As that wise ex-catcher with the New York Yankees and late philosopher said, "You can observe a lot by watching." And, as the Dalai Lama said, "When you talk, you are only repeating what you already know. But, if you listen, you may learn something new." By watching and listening, I was learning about things I would not have otherwise been able to do.

Engaging in the above experience was so enlightening that it led me to ask myself if it might be a good idea to also flip hamburgers in the agencies that are selling our policies. Spending a day by the side of an agency owner might awaken me to a better way our company could interact with their agency. Perhaps I could learn even more if I was side by side with an agency's CSR for eight or nine hours. I found that flipping hamburgers in my company and the agencies we served increased my knowledge. That knowledge helped me see a better path to pursue.

If you will flip some hamburgers, you'll engage in some things that will be eye opening. You'll learn from it. You'll improve from it. You'll be better as a result. Indeed, you'll accomplish what you didn't know you could.

Don't Travel Alone

It's said that life is a journey. Regrettably, many people take that trip by themselves. What if, unlike the many, you don't go alone? What if, as suggested in this chapter, you take some books with you? What if you take some people with brains and backbones with you? What if you even have some competitors ride along? And what if you flip a few burgers along the way?

I'm betting the trip will be less boring. The vehicle much faster. The car more comfortable. The sights more satisfying. The memories more meaningful. The destinations more delightful. And the best part is, instead of just viewing the landmarks left by those who preceded you, you may leave some landmarks of your own. You will have been where others said you couldn't go. You will have done the best you can't.

CHAPTER 9

BUSY SERVANT, NOT BIG SHOT

Answer Your Own Stinkin' Phone

THE PHONE RANG AND RANG and rang. Finally, Nick answered. While it was already 8:30 in the morning, it sounded like I had awakened Nick from a deep sleep. He had probably stayed up late watching election returns for the state house seat for which he was a candidate. Maybe he was catching up on lost sleep when I called him.

Just as I had won my race for a state senate seat, Nick had ended the night as a winner. I'm not so sure, however, that the word *winner* could be applied to his constituents. I say that because of the answer Nick gave to the question I asked after congratulating him on his victory. "Hey, Nick, what's the first thing you are going to do now that you have been elected to public office?" His answer: "I'm going to get me an unlisted phone number as quick as I can. Don't want to be bothered by a bunch of constituents calling me."

It was obvious to me that Nick and I had opposite opinions on the subject of constituents' calls. After my election victory, I had immediately contacted the phone company about installing a second line in my home. Remember, I'm an old fellow. There were no cell phones back then. People reached you by landlines in your home or business. I figured that I had, in effect, been hired by the voters. I would never avoid speaking with the person that hired me in business. He paid me and had a right to call me, speak with me in person, and communicate by handwritten notes, typed memos, or in any other way he so chose. I viewed my constituents in the same light. I worked for them. They had a right to call me. I felt obligated (and privileged, I might add) to make sure they could reach me without delays caused by a busy single-line phone. After all, I had chosen to become their servant—their public servant.

The word chosen in the sentence above is very appropriate. You see, in politics, there is rarely, if ever, such a thing as a draft. Candidates run for elective office because they want to. If candidates tell you they entered a campaign because gazillions of constituents petitioned them to run, they are exaggerating, if not outright lying. Personally, I've had more people beg me not to run for office than have ever begged me to run. But candidates like to feel needed, important, indispensable, and wanted. Their egos are massaged mightily by imagining that there is a gigantic groundswell of supporters anxious to anoint them.

Far too many elected officials view themselves as kings and queens. Therefore, the voters are mere subjects that should bow down to the exalted status of the elected office-holder. Some voters bear at least a little responsibility for elected officials feeling this way. They treat office-holders like gods. Thus, elected officials begin to think they are gods and deserve to be treated as such.

When constituents dared to deign my domain with a phone call, the vast majority of them were nervous, reluctant, and reticent. They often would stutter, stammer, and apologize for bothering me. Bother me! Why would I view it as being bothered? Why was an apology needed? After all, I had chosen to go to work for them. All they wanted to do was instruct me on how to do my job. Didn't they have that right?

Even the way my mail was addressed to me before I was elected was changed to denote how important I became after I was elected. Before the election, I was lucky to be addressed as "Mr." Stumbaugh. Most mail was addressed to just "Bud." After I was elected, my mail came to "The Honorable Bud Stumbaugh." Hey, I was honored to be elected, but that did not somehow make me honorable. In fact, it was a whole lot easier to be honorable before I was elected than after.

Another change that indicated I had become a bigwig after my successful campaign was the number of invitations I began to receive to sup with the high and the mighty. When highly regarded and well-known civic leaders, the heads of big companies, and the governor start inviting you to break bread with them, you can't help but think you are pretty popular. However, if you really want to gauge how popular you are, get defeated in an election. See how many invitations you receive then.

The truth is, for the first time in my life, I was being treated like royalty. I admit that it was wonderful. Remember, I grew up with an inferiority complex. My daddy left us when I was a year old. My momma supported four kids on minimum wages. That meant my clothes were not very stylish. My shoes were worn out. I wasn't invited to join classmates' social clubs. Since Momma didn't own a car, I couldn't date in high school. (You can't pick 'em up on a bicycle.) Thus, after being elected, to find myself accepted by the socially and politically acceptable was a magnificent moment in my life.

With no previous prestigious positions, no riches, no fame, no experience in elective or appointive office, I could hardly believe my good fortune. When I was sworn into the senate, I wondered, "How in the world did I get here?" I must confess that even though I doubted my worthiness, after getting to know other senators from around the state, I wondered, "How in the world did they get here?"

In spite of the early euphoria engendered by my election, my better nature reminded me that a senator is really a servant. So-called average people, the Janes and Johns that lived on lots like I lived on, began to use that second phone line I had installed. They really needed help with everyday problems. Their interests were not the special interests associated with undue favors for the few. Listening to their problems gave me proper perspective about the role I should play. I realized I needed to get my head out of the clouds and get down to some down-to-earth service/work.

Constituents weren't supposed to treat me like royalty. They were not supposed to put me on a pedestal or cater to me. It was my job to uphold and cater to them. Unlike movie stars, I could not bask in bliss. I could not because I was supposed to be a busy servant, not a big shot. Only if I had a servant spirit would I be able to achieve some things I would have not otherwise been able to do. It led me to doing the best I can't.

Keep in mind the above assertion that it was only when I adopted the servant spirit that I was able to accomplish things I could not otherwise have done. That's important to remember when I write below about one or two significant scenarios from my senate service. Otherwise, I'll come off as a big, boastful braggart. I have nothing to brag about because I know if I'm the turtle on top of the fence post, I certainly did not get there by myself.

The important point I'm trying to make is that significant achievements occurred because I acted upon the suggestions for service that were given to me. It was through the individuals and organizations that asked me to serve, and with their guidance, that I did some things I would never have done if they had not turned me into a servant who wasn't seeking their adulation but just trying to follow their lead.

For example, while I'm no medical doctor, geneticist, or scientist, Dr. Louis "Skip" Elsas, who had that trifecta of experience and talent, led me to indirectly talk and act like I was also experienced with all three. As a result, along with Dr. Elsas, I am credited with saving some thirty Georgia babies a year from becoming mentally disabled just three weeks after birth. Let me explain by quoting what Skip's family wrote about him after his death on September 16, 2012. This is just a little bit from his obituary.

"Skip was the driving force behind a statewide newborn screening health initiative, a pioneering and ultimate life-saving accomplishment that would become the flagship standard for newborn screening procedures across the world. Skip's development of new treatments for infants born with genetic metabolic disorders such as PKU, galactosemia and maple syrup urine disease gained him both national and international acclaim."

Dr. Elsas (we were always Skip and Bud to one another) was a part of a group called the Georgia Association for Retarded Children. In later years, the word *retarded* was deemed demeaning so is no longer used. Now, the proper nomenclature is *developmental disabilities*. In any case, this group knew I was accessible to not just the high and the mighty, but also to the burdened who could boast of few blessings. Skip and the association wanted to make me aware of genetic tests Skip had developed in the scientific labs of Emory University just a stone's throw from the Georgia State Capitol.

These were tests that could uncover six metabolic disorders that, if found within the first three weeks after birth, could be corrected with chemical treatments (medicines). If the disorders were not found within three weeks of birth and immediately corrected, the babies would end up with developmental disabilities. In other words, the clock was ticking toward doomsday in the most dramatic way possible.

Skip and the association wanted me to introduce a bill that would mandate that all newborns in Georgia must have their heels pricked and the resultant fluids tested for these six metabolic disorders before these babies reached the age of three weeks.

This was right up my alley. I always strove to be fiscally conservative and socially sensitive. Here was a clear chance to be both. There were several forms of developmental disabilities that could not be prevented or corrected. However, it was projected that thirty Georgia babies per year could be saved from these six metabolic disorders. Without discovery of their disorders within three weeks of their births, these babies' minds would not develop normally.

The cost to the state to assist each of these developmentally disabled babies would run some $30,000 per year. Thus, the state would save $900,000 per year by mandating tests of all newborns to find and save this thirty. With average life expectancy of thirty years for each developmentally disabled child, total savings over their lifetimes would accrue to some $27 million. Of course, more important than the money that would be saved were the heartache, stress, and difficulties the children and their families would avoid.

The happiest surprise birthday party I ever attended was ten years after my legislation had been passed by the senate and house and signed into law by the governor. Skip asked me to meet him at a conference room at Emory University for a slideshow he wanted me to see. When I walked into the room, there was no slideshow. Instead, it was a surprise celebration for me. Wow, I couldn't miss the big banner that read, "Georgia's Gene Team Turns Ten."

It was also impossible to miss the happy giggles, screams, and shouts of three hundred typical kids from one to ten years old who had gathered to celebrate their victory over developmental disabilities from which Skip's tests and my legislation had saved them.

Was saving three hundred kids something this nondoctor/nongeneticist/nonscientist could do? Absolutely no way. That is, not until I became a servant. Only then did I do what I otherwise would never have been able to do. I still treasure and keep in a prominent place the beautiful trophy they gave me the day "Georgia's Gene Team Turned Ten."

Almost as personally satisfying as the above was responding to a call from a constituent who phoned me at my capitol office. My secretary had answered the phone and told the caller I was on another line. She indicated that I would be off that call in just a minute or so and would pick up the constituent's line as soon as I finished. When I picked up the waiting call and said, "Hello, this is Bud," the constituent said she was pleased but shocked by the way we handled her call. First, my secretary did not ask, "May I tell him who is calling?" or, "What is the nature of your call?" I had a rule that my calls were never to be screened. Everybody and anybody was important enough for me to personally speak to.

My constituent had called her state representative and been screened. She had called some state agency heads and been screened. Apparently, those folks had forgotten who they worked for or just didn't care. She thought I cared. I certainly knew I was a servant elected to work for her. And I didn't play the big-shot senator card by declaring that title when I picked up the phone. It was, "Hello, this is Bud. How may I help you?" She made a point to tell me how pleased she was at my down-to-earth informality that put her at ease.

It surprised her even more when I told her I'd try to help with her request, but only if I could first visit with her and her husband at their home. You see, they wanted to adopt a child out of Georgia's foster-care system. Bureaucratic bungling had slowed the process to a standstill. I was willing to cut whatever red tape I could, but not before taking time to first determine whether they were decent human beings and whether their home seemed to be a clean, safe, and loving environment for a child. That needed to be done "officially" before an adoption could take place. But I was not going to ask the state to go through the vetting process until this nonprofessional/non-social worker made an "unofficial" judgment that the state should take the time to vet these would-be parents.

Obviously, to facilitate an adoption, a person must have a degree in social work and be certified or licensed in adoptive counseling. I did not qualify. Adoptions were something I couldn't facilitate. But because of my servant role, Harriet and Glen Littleton helped me accomplish their goal. Today, their daughter is grown and has given them a couple of grandchildren.

By the way, writing earlier about taking my senate phone calls without screening them reminds me to compliment two very high-level people who are not so puffed up with their own importance that they avoid callers.

When Jimmy Carter was president, his head of the Office of Management and Budget was a fellow named Bert Lance. I had what I thought was a bright idea about a new approach to budgeting our federal tax dollars. While I figured I'd never get to actually talk directly with Mr. Lance, who occupied a cabinet-level position and had been confirmed by the US Senate, I thought I'd at least try to relay my idea to someone in the department. So, around eight o'clock one morning, I telephoned the Office of Management and Budget. Low and behold, Mr. Lance himself answered the phone. He didn't use a secretary to screen out little ole me. Now, that's a busy servant, not a big shot!

Around eight o'clock on another morning, I needed to talk to US Senator Johnny Isakson. He represents some ten million Georgia constituents. While I knew he would be willing to talk individually with all ten million if they called, that would be a physical impossibility. Thus, his office had to inquire about the nature of the call when someone asked to personally speak with Johnny. This enabled them to transfer the call to an aide that was knowledgeable about the subject matter with which the caller needed help.

Understanding that process, when I called Senator Isakson's office and a man answered, I immediately said, "I know Senator Isakson can't talk with everybody, but if you'll please give him a note with my name and phone number on it, I know he will call me back. We know one another."

After patiently suffering through my entire spiel, the fellow on the other end of the phone said, "Bud, Bud, I don't need to call you back. This is Johnny." When I expressed amazement that he was personally picking up incoming phone calls, he explained to me that he occasionally did that as a means of staying in touch with regular, everyday kind of people. He understood that was who he worked for. Before his six-year senate term was complete, Johnny retired for health reasons, and he died a few months later. However, I will always proudly call him my senator.

Johnny's senate chief of staff also felt pretty positive about the senator. He was quoted in the June 30, 2021, *Atlanta Journal-Constitution* as saying, "I really got a chance to see someone who cares, someone who truly gave of himself and loves public service."

My belief that being a senator means being a servant rather than a big shot also applies to business. When I was CEO of AssuranceAmerica, more than one friend or acquaintance lamented that they worked for someone while I was fortunate to have three hundred people work for me. I always responded that nobody worked for me. Instead, I worked for each and every one of our associates.

For example, a salesperson asked me to visit with an insurance agency owner that the salesperson wanted to appoint to write AssuranceAmerica policies. The agency owner felt she already had enough companies with whom to write policies. I was happy to go to work for our salesperson and attempt to win over the agency owner. In effect, our salesperson became my sales manager assigning me to do a sales job.

Other times, associates might come to me about upgrading a printer or other piece of office equipment. In attempting to fulfill that need, I would work as their purchasing agent or maybe their financier. If associates needed more knowledge to become more effective, I worked as their trainer. The point is that if I was doing my job, that meant I was working for a lot of other people by performing tasks that would help them succeed. My job was to be a busy servant, not a corporate big shot.

We wanted our company's atmosphere to scream service and servant. Thus, we did not use titles of Ms. or Mr. Everyone was addressed by his or her first name. Neither did we call one another employer or employee. Instead, we referred to one another as colleagues or associates.

We did not view one person as more important than another. The janitor made less money than I because she had less education and no experience building a business. However, our company could not function if no one ever emptied the trash cans or vacuumed the carpets or dusted desks or cleaned toilets. The janitor and I had different functions, just like my hands and feet have different functions. And, just as my hands and feet are equally essential, the CEO and janitor are equally essential.

Viewing and treating everyone as equally important also influenced and impacted how I handled phone calls. Just as I did not allow screening of senate calls, I did not allow screening of company calls. To me, when a caller is asked, "May I tell him who is calling?" the message imparted is that some callers are important and some are not. I wanted all callers to feel important.

"Surely," you might say, "you don't take all the calls from all the salespeople who ask for you." Well, in addition to my desire that all callers feel important, there are at least three more reasons I take calls from salespeople. One, I believe in the Golden Rule. I want my salespeople to have all their calls answered. How can I want that kind of treatment for myself and my sales team but be unwilling to offer it to others?

In addition to the above, there are a couple of self-serving reasons for taking calls from salespeople. First, if the salesperson is really articulate, pleasant, convincing, and effective in other ways, I might want to hire her for my team. If I don't take the calls, I'll never know whether or not the person is effective.

Second, if I treat all sales or vendor callers like they are important, you can be sure that if my company chooses to use their products or services, we will get a lot better service than companies who treat them like they are a necessary but unpleasant bother. If you want the best prices and value, the quickest delivery, and the most and highest levels of attention, then interact with your vendors as if they are important partners in your business. They are!

By the way, if you really want to have an unusually wholesome and positive relationship with vendors, you should pay for both your part and their part of the lunches, dinners, and golf outings in which you engage. That way, you will never have a conflict of interest, and they will know you appreciate and value them as one of the cogs in the gears that keep your company running.

Now, back to the subject of accepting all phone calls. It is unwise for me to waste my time and unfair to waste a caller's time, so I'm not indicating I spend or you should spend an inordinate amount of minutes romancing every vendor on the other end of the phone.

If, for example, callers told me they wanted an appointment to discuss becoming our office products supplier, I'd always quickly thank them for their interest in AssuranceAmerica and then say something to the effect that all good salespeople like to deal with the decision-maker.

I'd let them know the decision-maker is so and so, who does not have to check with me to buy something, and I'd be happy to transfer the call to her. I'd also add that if we ended up doing business together, I'd like the caller to stick her head in my office so we could introduce ourselves the next time she visits us. You better believe this enhanced the quality of service from our vendors and helped our company achieve some things we would not have otherwise been able to achieve. It helped us do the best we can't.

Reaching out to people doesn't take long and will almost always make a positive impression. People may not remember what you say, but they never forget how you make them feel. That's why whenever I would walk through our company's reception area, no matter how big a hurry I was in, I'd greet whoever was sitting there. My message was pretty much the same each time. "Hi, my name is Bud, CEO and cofounder of AssuranceAmerica. I bet you are here to either sell us something or interview for a job. In either case, I wish us both the very best. What's your name?"

True story. One of our associates told me he took a job with our company even though he was offered a little more money from another employer. He said he did so because I had greeted him in the reception area and made him feel like he would be recognized and treated like an important individual if he joined us. Yep, it really will help you make a lot of things happen that would not otherwise happen if you choose to be busy serving rather than being a big shot that doesn't have time to make others feel valued.

Following are a few other true stories about servitude that hopefully will inspire you to live and work humbly to help others, no matter how lofty your status may be.

Henry (Hank) Aaron, who recently passed away, is so famous I don't need to tell you who he was. Yet, his fame, his wealth, his prestigious place in his profession never made him so haughty and arrogant that he could not serve others. Right after I had made a substantial investment in a company that was on the verge of bankruptcy or insolvency, I ran into Hank at one of Delta Airlines' waiting areas at the San Francisco Airport. Years before, we had met each other when we were both campaigning for the same candidate for governor of Georgia. We had not seen one another in several years, but Hank remembered me and we engaged in conversation.

Hank asked what I was doing. I told him I was struggling to save a company in which I had made a substantial investment. He asked if he could help in any way. Somehow, our dialogue turned to how his name might give my company credibility and open doors with prospective corporate customers if Hank was one of our board members. I acknowledged that his presence would be positively powerful. However, I told him I didn't have the financial wherewithal to pay board members. Hank told me he would serve for free for a year and would then need to leave the board. Keep in mind, Hank earned large fees for serving on other boards, but he was willing to serve on my board for free. There was nothing in it for him. He just wanted to help an old acquaintance (I can't honestly use the term "old friend," because we had not maintained contact after campaigning together).

Hank even went out of his way to accommodate strangers. Dave Hamrin of Atlanta was on a flight to Sarasota, Florida. Henry Aaron was on the same flight. Dave introduced himself, told Hank how much he enjoyed watching him play baseball, and asked a favor of him. Dave wanted Hank to help trick the friend that was picking up Dave at the airport into thinking Dave and Hank were longtime buddies.

Dave told the friend that was picking him up that he had never mentioned it before, but he and Hank were old friends. As Dave and his friend were leaving the baggage carousel with luggage in hand, they heard a loud voice yell, "Hey, Ham, see you later, buddy." It was Hank Aaron, smiling and waving like an old friend would do.

While Henry Aaron didn't do anything impossible by his generous gesture to Dave, another Henry, this one Henry Darby from North Charleston, South Carolina, is proof positive that a spirit of service can lead to impossible achievements. Darby was featured on a June 2021 episode of NBC's *The Today Show*. His story was so inspiring that it was later picked up by CNN, *People Magazine,* and other news outlets and publications.

Darby is principal of the local high school in North Charleston. More than half the students are at or below the poverty line. Darby had gone to one student's home to counsel with his parents. As he neared the front doorway, he could see through the windows, which had no curtains or blinds, that there were no beds in the bedrooms—just mattresses on the floors. In attempting to locate two other students, he found they lived under a bridge.

Darby decided to provide financial support to these and other students who were in desperate need. However, like most people, Darby had a mortgage, car payment, and other expenses that took most of his earnings. There wasn't money left over to help the kids with their needs. So Henry Darby got a part-time job from ten p.m. to seven a.m. three days a week stocking shelves at Walmart. He barely had time to change clothes and get to school after finishing his Walmart shift. He was earning only hourly pay at Walmart but was giving 100 percent of it to the needy kids.

No one who saw Mr. Darby stocking shelves knew he was the high school principal until a student saw him one night. The student told others what he had seen, and before long, Walmart's management was aware of who their part-time help was. They questioned him about his motivation for working part-time. Management was so inspired by his efforts to help deprived kids that Walmart made a $50,000 contribution to help Darby support these underprivileged high school students.

Henry Darby could never write a $50,000 check for needy kids. But he did. He could never be the focus of a TV show or a news magazine. But he was. Because he busied himself as a servant in a menial job, he was able to do the best he can't.

Giving financial support is not the only way to assist those in need. Helping the poor is not just about food and shelter. It may be boosting self-image, a feeling of importance, a smile, or a greeting tone that says someone is special rather than a subordinate subset of society.

The story of the student taking his first quiz in college very clearly makes that point. It was a pop quiz. The freshman said he was a very conscientious student and had breezed through the questions until he read the last one. "What is the name of the woman who cleans the school?"

Surely this was some kind of a joke. He had seen the woman several times and remembered she was short, light haired, and probably around fifty years old. But how in the world could he know her name?

He handed in his paper with a blank space following the last question. He asked the professor if the last question would count toward the test's grade. "Most definitely," said the professor. "In your career, you will meet lots and lots of people. They are all significant in their own way. They deserve your respect, your attention, and your care and concern, even if all you do is smile, say hello, and call their name."

The student says he has never forgotten that lesson. He also learned the cleaning lady's name was Betty.

Making the janitor feel good is, in my opinion, a healthy, heady, and high form of service. Working alongside the cleaning crew "ain't too shabby either." That's what New Jersey Congressman Andy Kim did on January 6, 2021, when some overzealous citizens stormed the US Capitol in an effort to halt the certification of a new president. After the capitol was cleared of protesters, Congressman Kim saw police officers putting pizza boxes and other debris in trash bags, so he asked for a bag and started to also clean the floors. Better than a big shot was he. A busy servant instead. An example worth immolating indeed.

What did Congressman Kim get by leaving his lofty perch in society's pecking order? Since newspeople picked up on what he had done, he got favorable publicity throughout his congressional district that he would never have been able to afford through advertising purchases. When I sell ten million copies of this book (hey, humor is healthier than hopelessness), he will have gained that many admirers he could never have imagined having.

Some skeptics will say Kim did not have a sincere servant spirit. He helped pick up trash just so he could get attention, appreciation, applause, and accolades that would assist him in his next campaign. That's possible, but since I don't own a motive meter by which I can measure his morals, all I can do is admire how tall he stood when he stooped to help police pick up trash off the capitol floors.

There is a story of supreme service and sacrifice I'd like to share because no one can doubt the sincerity of the little boy in it. This was relayed from a volunteer at a hospital who got to know a little girl who was suffering from a rare and deadly disease. Her best chance of recovery might lie with her five-year-old brother. He had almost miraculously recovered from the same disease and had developed the antibodies needed to fight his sister's sickness.

The doctor in charge explained that if the little boy would donate his blood to his sister, she would have a chance to live. The boy hardly hesitated. He told the doctor that if giving his blood would save his sister, he would do it.

The volunteer continued the story by telling how joyous everyone was as the transfusion took place and a healthy color almost immediately returned to the little girl's face. But then the brother's face grew pale and he asked in a trembling voice, "How long will it take for me to die?"

Perhaps because he was too young to fully understand what the doctor had explained to him, he thought he was going to have to give all his blood to his sister. In order for her to live, he thought he would have to die.

For most of us, being a busy servant instead of a big shot will never require the supreme sacrifice like the brother was willing to make. Service to others may be as simple as asking the waitperson at Waffle House her name and bragging about her service as you call her name. Maybe it's occasionally—I know this isn't reasonable every time— leaving a twenty-dollar or even a hundred-dollar tip. Maybe all it takes is getting off our high horse by cleaning up the coffee we spilled instead of asking the janitor or secretary to manage the mess we made. Maybe it's answering our own phone. Maybe it's sitting at the lunch table with the lowest-paid people in the company so they know you value them as fellow humans.

Now, if instead of being a busy servant, you want to be a big shot, there is no doubt you'll enjoy some creature comforts. When I was in the senate, I remember how some people would fawn over me, cater to me, and want to send me free tickets to ball games, boxes of candy for Christmas, pick up my tab at a restaurant, and give me lots of other gifts. Yes, if you play the role of big shot, you can get lots of stuff. But you won't *do* lots of stuff. That's one reason I had a personal policy of not accepting any gifts while I was in public office. I thought Robert Louis Stevenson's philosophy was the right approach to politics—really, to all of life. He said, "Don't judge each day by the harvest you reap, but by the seeds that you plant."

If you really want to get things out of life, a self-serving approach is not the most effective way to do so. Self-importance just won't work well. Indeed, being self-indulgent, self-obsessed, self-caring, or self-centered is not the path to getting things done that seem beyond your capabilities.

Zig Ziglar, who, before his death, was known as the czar of sales training and motivational speaking and was the author of thirty books, understood the best way to get things and the best way to get things done. He said, "I believe that you can get everything in life you want if you will just help enough other people get what they want."

You are not an ophthalmologist, so there is no way you can help the blind to see. Right? Wrong! Join the Lions Club. They are engaged in a lot of different service activities, but they focus on helping people who have problems with sight. They train dogs that lead the blind to walk places they could never traverse alone. They contribute to research universities that focus on optic-related projects. In the last year alone, the Lions Clubs contributed more than $8.3 million to vision-related grants. You'll do more than you ever dreamed you could possibly do if you commit to serve through a civic club like the Lions.

You aren't capable of providing college scholarships to five people in a small town like the one in which I live. Right? Wrong! Our local newspaper, *The Dahlonega Nugget*, recently ran a story of how the local women's club did exactly that. Their members collected donated items to sell, sponsored barbecue suppers for which the public purchased tickets, and rented space in their club's headquarters to vendors with goods to sell at town fairs, and used the proceeds from all this to help kids finance their college education. Yes, serve and you can send students to school.

You are not a management consultant, so you can't help someone improve her business. Right? Wrong! Join your local chamber of commerce and you'll end up helping more businesses than you ever thought you would.

Dear Abby told a writer to her column who felt he was useless, accomplishing nothing, and wasn't capable of doing anything worthwhile that he could change all that by logging onto volunteermatch. org and choosing to serve one of their recommended causes. Abby understands what a lot of self-centered egotist have not yet learned. You are more likely to do what you thought you couldn't do if you are a busy servant rather than a big shot.

CHAPTER 10

WHY YOU SHOULD DO THE BEST YOU CAN'T

Death Will Never Do Us Part

You WANT TO KNOW WHAT is more difficult than sailing west to get east? What's tougher than running a sub-four-minute mile? What's scarier than walking across the Grand Canyon on a wire rope or even a 2x8 plank? For me, it's writing a book.

You see, writing a book is something I can't do. This last chapter, if I don't drop dead before it is finished, proves a person can do the best she or he can't. It should prove to you that the impossible is possible, because it is just not possible for me to write a book. Yet, if you are reading this, you know I have done it.

More than thirty years ago, after giving one of my motivational speeches before a large crowd, a fellow came up to me and said I ought to write a book that espouses what I had just encouraged hundreds of people to do. "Why not," he said, "reach thousand or even tens of thousands of people with your message?" He pointed out that I might never speak before a hundred thousand people, but that I could write to that many or more. Others, including my colleagues at work, have urged me to write what they have heard me say in speeches, seminars, training classes, or in one-on-one sessions giving counsel, instructions, and encouragement to individuals. Why did it take thirty years for me to do what so many have suggested?

Knowing I've had ADHD since my youth, and I haven't grown out of it, I realized writing a book would be a terribly tough task. Since concentration is a major problem for me, how in the world could I possibly string words out enough to complete a coherent, comprehensible chapter, much less a book? I can't focus well enough to stick with a different subject matter for each chapter. I never use notes when giving a speech, so how can I, in effect, write a notebook? I'm a bit of a country bumpkin who has no training in how to professionally phrase a point I want to make. I can think it, but I can't write it. I struggle to remember when and where to use an adverb or an adjective. Is it or is it not okay to end a sentence with a preposition? Should there be concise, choppy short sentences or long and winding words woven together?

I don't know the answers to all those questions. As a result, I can't write a book. But these pages you are perusing prove otherwise. That should instill in you the confidence it takes to do the best you can't. If I can do what I can't, you can do what you can't.

So what can't you conquer, but will anyhow? Is it something from the long list of can'ts I catalogued in a couple of other chapters? Or is it something you need to add to my list? What is it you have *really* wanted to do but thought or said, "I can't?"

Almost everyone has a Mt. Everest. A looming challenge that conjures those four forbidden letters of the alphabet (*c a n t*) plus an apostrophe. You are probably thinking of something right now. It is
_____ (fill in the blank).

This book is not written to provide a recreational pause in someone's routine. The goal is to get every single reader to choose from the lists of can'ts I've provided, or some other can't each respective reader provides, and plan a way to do what can't be done. After that can't is accomplished, the goal is to choose another one and also achieve it. Remember, earlier chapters suggest the processes, procedures, and principles to follow if you really want to do the best you can't.

It starts with starting. For me, I had to quit saying I hope to write a book "someday." I decided to practice what I had been preaching. Set a specific day and time to start, because "someday" is not definite enough. I set timelines and deadlines to begin and end each chapter of this book.

Then I had to overcome fear. My fear of printing thousands of books and selling only hundreds was overcome by remembering that if I didn't reach the moon, I might at least fall among the stars. Maybe I'd sell only a few books. So what if I lost money on a stockpile of books that didn't sell very well? It would hurt my bank account at least a little, but it wouldn't bankrupt me.

I knew hard work, even if it meant hundreds more hours than anyone else would take to complete a book, was the answer. Not intellect. Not experience. Not riches. Not built-in advantages. Not influential sources. Just good, old-fashioned hard work. And then some.

So, other than the desire to see you, dear reader, tackle and accomplish an impossible task, why did I take the time and go to the trouble of writing this book? What did I hope the real end result would be?

Maybe my main motivation is encompassed in a truism out of Ben Franklin's *Poor Richard's Almanack*. He said, "If you don't want to be forgotten soon after your death, then write a book worth reading or lead a life worth writing." Fact is, I really want to positively influence my kids and grandkids, not only today, but for many tomorrows after

I no longer physically exist. I'd like to change them and the world for the better, even after I'm no longer living in it.

In case I didn't "lead a life worth writing," I'm hopeful I've "written a book worth reading." A book that will be the positive influence I deeply desire to always have on my kids, grandkids, and the world. This book is my means of leaving a legacy. My will will distribute my valuables. This book will distribute my values. Hopefully, they are more meaningful than money and other material means combined.

The truth is, whether or not I write a book, I will be sharing my values, good or bad, even after I die. I'll be sending messages to the living after my body is buried or burned. So will you. You will communicate from your grave.

The traditional marriage ceremony uses the phrase, "Til death do us part." No matter how positive or negative a relationship, whether it be a marriage relationship, a business relationship, an athletic relationship, a neighborhood relationship, a religious relationship, or a civic relationship, death won't end the relationship. It's not "til death do us part." Indeed, it's "death will never do us part."

Yes, you'll talk from your grave. I don't mean you'll speak through some hocus-pocus, spirit-induced spell or séance. Read on and you'll understand how your funeral is far from the final time you'll share food for thought.

Knowing he was days from death on a tragic trek to the South Pole in 1912, Captain Robert Falcon Scott wrote a letter that opened with this salutation, "To my widow." He told her of his love and gave advice to her and their three-year-old son. The letter was recovered the year after Scott froze to death. Dead, but a year later, he was still speaking with his wife and son.

In the New Testament book of Hebrews (chapter 11), it tells how Able pleased God more than his brother Cain, who had killed Able. Because of his better example, Hebrews 11: 4 (RSV) says of Able, "He died ... but he is still speaking." Like Able, someday we will all die. Yet we will continue to communicate, if not through writings like Captain Scott's letter, or my book, then through the examples (good or bad) others remember us setting while we were alive.

If nothing else will motivate you to do the best you can't, the fact that, even after death, you will still be talking to your family, your friends, your neighbors, your coworkers, your shoeshine person, your bank teller, your house cleaner, your teachers, your part of the world, no matter how small or large, should encourage you to do the best you can't. You should want all these people to marvel at how much you overcame to do the difficult and practice the positive. You should want them to be inspired by what you are saying from your grave.

After you die, what will your kids and others hear you say?

Will it be, "Take care of your body by not smoking, not overdrinking, not overeating," because you are exhibiting an excellent example right now?

Will they hear you say, "Be courteous, kind, respectful, not only to powerful people, but to the waitress at the hole-in-the-wall café down the street and the janitor at school," because they see you make a special effort to make these people feel good?

Will they hear you say, "Treat all races and ethnic groups equally like you want to be treated," because they never heard you tell a demeaning joke, never heard you utter racial slurs, and never saw bigotry in your actions?

Will they hear you say, "Work hard, don't complain about your employer, and be grateful you have a paycheck," because they see you smile when you leave for work and when you get back home from work each day, and they don't hear you gripe about your boss?

Will they hear you say, "Speak in soft and loving tones to your spouse and your children," because you never put them down and express exasperation even when they mess up from time to time, as all humans will do?

Will they hear you say, "Nurture nature," because they saw you save a baby bird that had fallen from its nest?

Will they hear you say, "Volunteer for a good cause," because you joined the Alzheimer's Association even though no one in your family has any kind of dementia?

Will they hear you say, "Live on only 80 percent of your paycheck," because they saw you save or invest 10 percent and give away 10 percent to worthy causes?

Will they hear you say, "Support decent candidates for public office," because at each election time, they saw you put a candidate's yard sign in front of your house?

Will they hear you say, "Don't let just the rich and special-interest groups financially assist political campaigns," because they saw you write a ten-, fifty-, or hundred-dollar check to a candidate or two each election cycle?

Will they hear you say, "Help the helpless," because you rescued a cat or dog from a kill shelter?

Will they hear you say, "Do the right thing, even if you won't get caught when you don't," because they saw you contact someone to return their wallet full of money after you found it along the roadside?

Will they hear you say, "Don't be a sullen and serious old grouch," because they saw you sometimes laugh so hard you had to gasp for breath?

Will they hear you say, "The important things in life are not things," because they saw you invest not only in money-making mechanisms but also in causes, charities, and community?

Will they hear you say, "Don't be a know-it-all," because they saw you use your ears more than your mouth?

Will they hear you say, "Take calculated risks rather than stay stuck in the silo of sameness," because they never saw you succumb to the sweet songs of safety and security?

Will they hear you say, "Be reliable and keep your word," because of the two approaches you took toward promises? One: you made very few. Two: you kept the ones you made.

Will they hear you say, "Self-discipline is possible," because you quit smoking after seventeen years of two packs a day?

Will they hear you say, "Self-discipline is possible," because you gave up second helpings and desserts in order to lose forty pounds?

Will they hear you say, "Don't hesitate to ask for help if a problem is so entrenched there is not enough self-discipline to overcome it," because, depending on whatever the problem was, you freely disclosed that you joined AA to assist you, or you sought anger-management intervention, or marriage counseling, or … or … or … ?

Will they hear you say, "Even a single parent who doesn't have the time or money for a college education can attain one anyway," because they saw you start with just one little Saturday class at the local community college?

Will they hear you say, "Not everyone needs to think and act like you think and act," because they saw you accept other tastes, customs, and cultures without feeling the necessity to convince others that your way is the only right way to think and act?

Will they hear you say, "There are times to bend and be flexible, and there are times to take a stand as strong as steel," because they saw you compromise programs you preferred but never principles you professed?

Will they hear you say, "I can't do that *yet*," rather than, "I can't do that," because they saw a healthy curiosity to expand beyond current capabilities?

Will they hear you say, "You are never too old to start something new," because they saw you go to dance classes, art classes, drone-flying classes, or something similar after you were sixty-five years old?

Will they hear you say, "Being better than others is not the most meaningful goal," because they saw you give great effort to be better than yourself?

Will they hear you say, "There is something more important than the security of a paycheck," because you quit a job that required you to make a false pitch for a flawed product?

Will they hear you say, "There is something more important than the security of a paycheck," because you took a substantial pay cut to start your own business?

Will they hear you say, "It's better not to have all the answers," because they saw you use a lack of knowledge as a good excuse for collaboration?

Will they hear you say, "There is a warmer way to communicate than modern technology often offers," because they saw you take the time to compose and mail handwritten notes to thank people, to congratulate and comfort them and to encourage them?

Will they hear you say, "You can accomplish tomorrow what you can't today," because they saw that you never gave up but kept trying, even after being defeated time and time again?

Will they hear you say, "Be sure your wisest words are those you don't say," because they did not hear you rant and rave uncontrollably when provoked?

Will they hear you say, "Don't make yourself miserable by whining about what you don't have," because you showed gratitude for a healthy child, a spouse who loves you, a roof over your head, enough energy to work, eyes to see, ears to hear, and opportunities to improve your lot in life?

Will they hear you say, "The focus for friendship should not be socio-economic status," because you formed relationships based on individuals' decency, positive personalities, and, sometimes, just their need for an amiable association?

Will they hear you say, "Merit should be the basis for hiring and promoting, but never overlook the often overlooked," because you proactively sought qualified people from other races and cultures before you employed the more easily found candidates?

Will they hear you say, "You don't have to file lawsuits, engage in heated shouting matches, or do dirty deeds to get even, even with extremely egregious enemies," because they saw you turn the other cheek, try tolerance, nicely negotiate, and when all else failed, favor forgiveness instead of fights?

Will they hear you say, "You are not poor when you are broke," because they knew you had no money but saw you were rich in respect and flourished from favor of family and friends?

The above are some positive messages people can hear you say after you die, if you incorporate them into your life today. You can do that even if they are attributes you don't now have and things you can't now do. If you are alive and aware enough to read this book, you probably have enough time left to mold a more meaningful message to give from your grave than what you would give if you had died yesterday.

Just remember, your destiny is not determined until you die. Your current circumstance and condition are not cast in concrete. Your self is not yet set in stone. So start working today on what you and others think you can't do. Achieve it now so when you are gone, others will hear you say they can do the impossible because you proved that doing the impossible is possible.

When you were born, you were crying and everyone around you was smiling. Hopefully, when you die, you will be smiling and everyone around you will be crying. But you want their tears to be temporary. They can be, if the message you send after you die is that it is possible to overcome obstacles, win the war against weaknesses, and then exceed expectations because everyone remembers you did the best you can't.

ABOUT THE AUTHOR

Courtesy of The Dahlonega Nugget

Bud Stumbaugh now owns a silver spoon but didn't grow up with one in his mouth. In fact, he sometimes had no spoon at all. His school drop-out mom found it difficult to put food on the table for him and his three sisters on the minimum wages she earned after his father left when Bud was one.

At nine years old Bud picked cotton for a penny a pound to help buy school clothes. In high school Bud couldn't date because his mom didn't own a car and, as he said, "You can't pick 'em up on a bicycle."

He grew up with an inferiority complex which had him stuck on scared. But Bud got unstuck. He decided he didn't like being disadvantaged and defeated. He worked his way through college and now has an honorary Ph.D. on top of his bachelor's degree. He overcame his fear of public speaking and became a motivational speaker before conventions and business, religious, civic and political groups. He also served 8 terms in the Georgia State Senate. And he built a company from zero to $200 million in ten years.

Some feel Bud did what seemed impossible. His book will inform you how to also do what seems impossible and will inspire you to tackle the task today.

You may contact Bud on his cell (404-317-5991) or his personal email (stumb1234@gmail.com).